PORTRAIT OF THE PAST

Portrait of the Past

A Pictorial Glance

At

Lower Johnson County, Tennessee;

And the Elk, Roan & Watauga Valleys

Watauga Valley, Fish Springs, Carter County, Tennessee 1942
(Courtesy: Glenn Elliott)

Roan Valley, Neva Post Office, Neva, Johnson County, Tennessee
(Compiler Photo)

A Very Special
Thank You
To Those Who Provided
Photographs and Permitted
Their Use in This Book

Acknowledgements are listed with each
Individual Picture

Thanks To:
Nancy Tester, Roland Tester, Rob Tester,
Carolyn Tester Wagner &
Juanita Tester Wilson

Portrait of the Past

A Pictorial Glance

at

Lower Johnson County, Tennessee;

And the Elk, Roan & Watauga Valleys

Compiled and Written By Charles Herman Tester
ISBN 978-0-578-09041-2
Published by
LUEM PUBLISHERS
147 Earl Light Circle
Jonesborough, Tennessee 37659
423/753-6961

testdbprin@aol.com

Books by C.H. Tester

Title	ISBN	Copyright
Butler: Old, New and Carderview	9780615154671	2006
Johnson County Tennessee 1930 Census VI	9780615243351	2002
Johnson County Tennessee 1930 Census VII	9780615241524	2002
Carter County Tennessee 1930 Census	9780578014753	2009
Companion Book Johnson County 1930 Census		2002
Portrait of the Past	9780578090412	2011

Portrait of the Past

A Pictorial Glance
at
Lower Johnson County, Tennessee;
And the Elk, Roan & Watauga Valleys

Copyright 2011
by
Charles Herman Tester

All Rights Reserved
No part of this book may be reproduced or utilized in any form or by any means, electronic or mechanical, including photocopying, recording, or by any information or storage or retrieval system, without permission in writing from the Publisher

1900 Watauga Valley, Laurel Fork, Watauga County, North Carolina
Bee Hives of Oliver Jerome Presnell
(Courtesy: Juanita Tester Wilson)

1930 Roan Valley, Butler, Johnson County, Tennessee
Whiting Lumber Company
(Courtesy: George Walker)

Preface

The Tennessee Valley Authority planned the Watauga Project in the late 1930's. Approved in 1941 it was delayed by World War II. Finally it was completed and the gates were closed on the Watauga Dam December 1, 1948. Subsequently the waters of the Watauga Lake flooded the lower end of Johnson County, Tennessee and the Roan Creek, Elk River and Watauga River Valleys by October, 1949.

This vast area contains thousands of acres of flat land, hills, small and large hollows and mountainsides. Many homes and other buildings were moved by the property owners, while most, along with large mounds of cut timber, were razed and burned by the Tennessee Valley Authority. The haste of the leaders of the Tennessee Valley Authority lay to waste the manmade structures and natural resources of the area so that power production, the real reason for the Watauga Project, could get back on track.

Many of the photographs presented in this book represent life as it was 'before the lake'. Many affected families pictured in this book had resided here long before Tennessee became a state in 1796.

The Watauga River begins on the Grandfather Mountain in North Carolina and just after reaching Tennessee it now becomes the Watauga Lake. Roan Creek runs from the Snake Mountain near Trade, Tennessee and Zionville, North Carolina. The upper and middle valleys of the Roan remain intact while the lower Roan Valley, where Butler was located, is under the waters of the lake. The Elk River tumbles down the Stone Mountain from North Carolina and enters Tennessee just above Elk Mills. Just past this locale this stream now also becomes the lake.

Maps are included to remind or inform the reader as to the geographic location of the area from which these photographs were collected.

Best wishes to you for an enjoyable experience with this book.

C.H. Tester
Sulphur Springs, Tennessee
Summer 2011

1870's Watauga Valley, Sugar Grove, Johnson County Tennessee
Home of Solomon Quincy Dugger and Nancy King Dugger
(Courtesy: Juanita Tester Wilson)

1940's Elk Valley, Sugar Hollow Road, Buntontown, Johnson County Tennessee
(Compiler Photo)

Introduction

Fred R. Barnard is quoted as saying in the <u>Printer's Ink</u> March 10, 1927
'One Picture is Worth a Thousand Words'

This is possibly true. Old photographs portray where we have been and who we are. Photographs provide insight to generations of school, church and work groups, family reunions, recreational and athletic participants and other individual, social and family settings.

Photographs capture and preserve segments of life and document moments cherished forever by the subjects, their families, friends and strangers. Looking at photographs which portray the distant or recent past in good or poor quality is an activity enjoyed by many.

Unfortunately these photographs which provide so much joy and so many learning opportunities are very destructible. They are easily destroyed, lost, misplaced or forgotten. Many photographs preserved through one or more generations have been, through carelessness or wanton destructive behavior, lost to all future generations.

Preservation of precious old photographs for the special feeling one gets when opening a picture album is the reason for compiling this large book of photographs.

Many of the photographs in this book list the name(s) of the person(s), the approximate year and the general location. Some acquired photographs are unidentified and will be featured in a future photograph book similar to this one. Other good quality photographs are extant and are already included in that second volume.

**1940's Butler, Johnson County, Tennessee
Mr. Peter B. Elliott Home (Courtesy: Glenn Elliott)**

**Julius Dugger Cemetery, Sugar Grove, Watauga Lake
Grave Stone for John Dugger, Sr and Mary Dugger and the 'Twenty Duggers"
(Compiler Photo)**

Roan Valley, Stout Branch 1904: Mr. John Henry Matheson (1875-1968) and wife Catherine Stout Matheson (1877-1956) and daughter Sallie Alice (1902-1989) (Courtesy: Nancy Fritts Tester)

Watauga Valley, Sugar Grove 1916: Delores (Dee) Cable (1914-2010) (Courtesy: Dee Tester)

Roan Valley, Butler 1945: l-r Lawrence Dugger, Flenoy Medley, Amy Dugger Medley, Glenn Walker, Leona Dugger Walker and Bert Lunceford (Courtesy: George Walker)

Roan Valley, Vaughtsville, Maymead 1930's: Thomas Worley (Courtesy: Nancy Fritts Tester)

David Baker and wife, Mary Cable Baker (Courtesy: Dee Cable Tester)

Roan Valley, Rock Springs School 1950's: Mr. R.D. Campbell (Compiler Photo)

Hopper Creek, Doe Mountain, Neva 1930: Robert Brownlow (Bob) Fritts (1903-1969) son of George Washington Fritts (1872-1955) and Nettie Lunceford Fritts (1878-1955). All interred in the Pleasant Grove Baptist Church Cemetery, Roan Valley, Maymead. (Courtesy: Nancy Fritts Tester)

**Doeville, 1950's: Karl Pleasant and wife Louise Tucker Pleasant and son, Mike
(Courtesy: Louise Tucker Pleasant)**

Roderick Butler (Judge) Pleasant (1884-1937) and Vena Price Pleasant (1890-1970) and the 'OK' family of Doeville in 1930. Children are Kyle, King, Karl, Kale, Keys, Klan, Ola, Ova and Ona. Mr. and Mrs. Pleasant are interred in the Pleasant-Howard (Rambo) Cemetery at Doeville on Dugger Hollow Road.
(Courtesy: Louise Tucker Pleasant)

Roan Valley, Stout Branch 1930's: D. L. Stansberry (Courtesy: Dan Stansberry)

Roan Valley, Maymead 1930's: James Worley (Courtesy: Nancy Fritts Tester)

Butler City School 1926 Primer, First and Second Grade Students. Peggy O'Neil, Teacher 1st row l-r Hazel McElyea, Fred Mary, Jack McQueen, Robert Nave, Helen Ward, Edwina McQueen, LaVerne Shuffield, Marjorie Moore, Helen Neatherly, Verna Lee Wolfe, Dovie Eggers, Helen Shuffield 2nd row l-r JC Norris, Lacy Stout, Edwin DeVault, Louise Tucker, Vernell Courtner, Doris Atwood, Lois Burton, Fay Norris, Billy Joe Lineback, Anne VonCannon 3rd row l-r Lacy Pilk, Earl Presnell, Fleenor Stout, Ellis Tucker, Louise Birchfield, Elana Campbell, Lida Cable, Vivian Reed, Christine Whitehead. (Courtesy: Louise Tucker Pleasant)

Butler, 1940's: Mary Alice McQueen (Courtesy: Bob White)

Newark, Delaware 1940's: Una Fritts Glick (Courtesy: Una Fritts Glick)

**Watauga River, Cowantown 1920's:
Cora Burton (1890-1971).
Interred in the Cable Cemetery,
Sugar Grove, Watauga Lake
(Courtesy: Martha Bunton Query)**

Doyle Wilson (Courtesy: Juanita Tester Wilson) Veril Wilson

Roan Valley, Dry Hill, Duncan Hollow
1920's:
Bernice and Louise Greenwell
(Courtesy: Dan Stansberry)

Roan Valley, Mill Creek 1948: front Edwin Matheson, back l-r Sallie Matheson Fritts, Margie Ann Matheson, Beatrice Simcox Matheson (Courtesy: Claude Matheson)

Watauga Valley, Sugar Grove 1918: Nettie Cable (Courtesy: Juanita Tester Wilson)

Midway 1950: Steve Tester (Courtesy: Dee Tester)

Hopper Branch, Doe Mountain, Neva 1920's: home of George and Nettie Lunceford Fritts. l-r Wiley Fritts, Una Fritts and Rosa Fritts. (Courtesy: Nancy Fritts Tester)

Roan Valley, Stout Branch 1940: l-r Lois Fritts, Nancy Fritts, Barton Matheson, James Fritts, Dwight Fritts
(Courtesy: Claude Matheson)

Roan Valley, Mill Creek 1900: John Linville (Jack) Church (1859-1914) (Courtesy: Margaret Cress)

Roan Valley, Mill Creek 1944: Earl and Edwin Matheson (Courtesy: Claude Matheson)

Roan Valley, Neva 1920: Mr. John Roby Stout and wife Mae McCulloch Stout
(Courtesy: Claude Matheson)

**John and Catherine Stout Matheson Family, Stout Branch, Neva 1940: Clockwise from left: Beatrice, Edwin, Sallie Fritts, Harold Fritts, Earl, Raleigh, John, Catherine, Norma, Claude, Lois Fritts, Jim Fritts, Dwight Fritts, Nancy Fritts, Jean
(Courtesy: Claude Matheson)**

Watauga Lake, Hank's Dock 1950: Nelson Tester (Courtesy: Juanita Tester Wilson)

Children of Eli Finley and Camoline Presnell Tester, 1950 Tester Reunion, , Elk Valley, Sugar Hollow: Front l-r: Coy, Ben, Lewis, Nelson 2nd l-r: Rilda, Aner, Ida, Ruth, Ruby, Mae Back l-r: Pierce, Earl, Luke, Howard. Eli Finley (1872-1954) and Camoline (1880-1947) are interred in the Andrews/Tester Cemetry, Sugar Hollow, Watauga Lake. In 2011, Howard, age 86 and Ruth, 91, are living. (Courtesy: Dee Tester)

Watauga Valley, Sugar Grove, 1925: William (1869-1930) and Ella (1876-1940) Anderson Cable. They are interred in the Cable Cemetery, Sugar Grove, Watauga Lake, Butler.
(Courtesy: Dee Cable Tester)

Watauga Valley, Old Watauga River Road, Sugar Grove, 1900: Benjamin D. Cable (1835-1918) and Susannah Simerly Cable (1836-1920). Interred Cable Cemetery, Sugar Grove. And daughters Mary (Baker) and Levisa (Smith). (Courtesy: Juanita Tester Wilson)

Luke Lee Tester (1911-1967) and Dee Cable Tester (1914-2010) at their Midway Service Station, Grill and Grocery, Watauga Lake, Butler, 1948: Luke and Dee also began and operated Midway Boat Dock. They are interred in the Bradley Cemetery on a hill overlooking Little Dry Run, Watauga Lake and Midway Community including their home. Their children (and spouse) are Charlene Laws (Chalmas) Charles Herman (Nancy Fritts), Juanita Wilson (Jack Jr.), Carolyn Wagner (Bobby), Pat Icenhour and Steven Kent Tester. Robert Lee was born and died in 1942. Luke's parents were Eli Finley and Camoline Presnell Tester. Luke was born in Watauga County North Carolina at Laurel Fork. Dee's parents were William and Ella Anderson Cable. Dee was born in Johnson County at Sugar Grove. Luke was one of fourteen children (Aner, Coy, Pierce, Earl, Ben, Ida, Luke, Nelson, Lewis, Ruby, Ruth, Mae and Howard). Dee was one of eight (Nettie, Dewey, Annie, Ordie, Verdie, Dee, Alta and Alma). Two of Luke's siblings are living in 2010, Ruth, age 90 and Howard, age 85. Dee died in 2010, the last of her family. Luke worked at North American Rayon Corporation from the early 1930's until the mid 1950's. He then worked for Johnson County in the bus garage and drove a school bus. Dee ran the store and grill and worked as a waitress and as a domestic. They farmed on a small scale throughout their marriage.
(Courtesy: Dee Tester)

**Luke Lee Tester and Delores (Dee) Cable Tester on their wedding day 1933
Sugar Hollow, Elk River.: Married at the gate leading to the Elijah Dugger farm
by Reverend Peter Lee Lyons, pastor of Mountain View (Bakers Gap) Baptist Church.
(Courtesy: Dee Tester)**

Hopper Creek, Doe Mountain, Neva 1911: George Washington Fritts (1871-1955) and Nettie Lunceford Fritts (1878-1955). Interred in the Pleasant Grove Church Cemetery, Maymead, Neva. Children: (clockwise from left) Rettie, Brady, Charlie, Bob, Wiley and Lillie. (Courtesy: Nancy Fritts Tester)

Doe Creek 1959: Jack Wilson, Sr. & Tennessee State Record Rainbow Trout
(Courtesy: Juanita Tester Wilson)

Paris, 1945: Barton Matheson and Claude Matheson (Courtesy: Claude Matheson)

Roan Valley, Crackers Neck, Neva 1941: Lawrence Fritts and Kenneth Fritts, sons of John Fritts and Dorothy Simcox Fritts, (Courtesy: Nancy Fritts Tester)

Dwight Fritts (1936-1999)
Interred in the Dyson Grove Baptist Church Cemetery
(Courtesy: Nancy Fritts Tester)

**Christman Day, 1938 at Midway home of Luke and Dee Tester: Clockwise from left: Mae Tester, Dee Tester, Ruby Tester Trivette, Margie Lewis Tester, Nelson Tester, Herman Tester, Howard Trivette, Charlene Tester.
(Compiler Photo)**

Ruby Tester Trivette (Courtesy: Juanita Tester Wilson)

Midway 1937: Luke and Herman Tester (Courtesy: Dee Tester)

**Roan Valley, Old Roan Creek Road, 1940: Juanita Tester, Herman Tester, Luke Tester
(Courtesy: Linda Tester Hollaway)**

Roan Valley, Midway Dock, Watauga Lake: 1st 'drawdown' 1954, Luke Tester and son, Steve Tester
(Courtesy: Dee Tester)

Midway, 1950's: June Ellen Lewis & Steve Tester

**Midway, 1937: Lena Forrester holding Juanita Tester
(All Photos Courtesy: Juanita Tester Wilson)**

Midway, Old Little Dry Run Road 1944:
Dee Tester holding Pat, Carolyn on left, Juanita on right, Tyke out front
Daniel Bradley barn in left background, Stacy Grindstaff barn in right background,
Big Dry Run Mountain in center background
(Courtesy: Dee Tester)

Midway 1942: Juanita Tester, Carolyn Tester (Courtesy: Juanita Tester Wilson)

**Roan Creek Valley, 1945: Charlene Tester, Juanita Grindstaff, Lorene Forrester, Pearl Morley
(All Photos Courtesy: Juanita Tester Wilson)**

Doc and Texie Forrester Home Midway 1938: l-r Herman Tester, Juanita Tester, Lorene Forrester

Watauga Valley, Sugar Grove 1919: Mr. Charles Monroe McCloud (1886-1979) and Mrs. Flossie (Ara) Dugger McCloud (1894-1951) and daughter, Crystal. Mr. and Mrs. McCloud are interred in the Sugar Grove Cemetery, Watauga Lake, Butler. (Courtesy: Thomas C. McCloud)

**Watauga Valley, Laurel Falls, Watauga County, NC, 1912: Ben, Luke, and Ida Tester
(Courtesy: Luke Tester)**

Roan Valley 1940's: Clifton DeLoach and Una Fritts (Courtesy: Una Fritts Glick)

**Watauga Valley, Sugar Grove, 1945: Albert Cable, son of Dewey Cable and Josie Laws Cable
(Compiler Photo)**

Roan Valley, Midway, 1955: Nancy Fritts and Herman Tester (Compiler Photo)

, Roan Valley, Duff and May Dugger home, 1935:
Charles and Anna Dugger
(Courtesy: Anna Dugger Adkins)

Neva, Doe Mountain,, Fire Tower Road 1935: Rosa and Una Fritts (Courtesy: Una Fritts Glick)

Butler Springs, Old Watauga River Road, 1947: Karolyn Ketron. (Compiler Photos)

Butler, 1940's: Jack and Bill Ward (Courtesy: Bobby Jack Ward)

John Fritts (Courtesy: Una Fritts Glick)

Butler 1940's: Edna Earle Honeycutt, Valedictorian of Watauga Academy Class of 1948 (last class)
(Compiler Photo)

Watauga Valley, Cowantown 1939: clockwise from lower right: Frank Burton, Matilda Burton Tucker, Mary Burton Miller, Cora Burton, Ellen Burton Bunton (Courtesy: Florence Tucker)

**Herbert Tucker, Matilda Burton Tucker, Louise Tucker Pleasant, Florence Tucker
Mike Pleasant (Courtesy: Florence Tucker)**

Roan Valley, Butler: Isaac W. Courtner (Courtesy: Mary Walker Ward)

Roan Valley, Butler, Butler City School Playground, 1941: Florence Tucker and Paul Riley
(Courtesy: Florence Tucker)

**Watauga Valley, 1939: Frank Burton (1857-1942)
Interred in the Butler Memorial Cemetery
(Courtesy: Florence Tucker)**

Roan Valley near Maxwell Siding, 1940: Loss Lewis and his dog on soon-to-be-destroyed Southern Railroad tracks. First railroad trestle above Butler was a few hundred feet from this location. That and hundreds of other trestles, tracks and bridges were destroyed in the August 1940 flood.(Courtesy: Linda Tester Hollaway)

Roan Valley, Southern Railroad tracks, 1940: brother and sister Margie Lewis Tester and Beryl Lewis.
(Courtesy: Linda Tester Hollaway)

Midway, 1950: Jim Kimberlin (front) W. T. Bradley, Larry and Doug Bradley on haystack and Charles Bradley at right almost out of photo. (Courtesy: Juanita Tester Wilson)

**Butler 1920's: Florence Tucker, Louise Tucker
(Courtesy: Louise Tucker Pleasant)**

Roan Valley, 1930's: Anna Dugger. Little Dry Run (Bradley) Mountain in center background, Duff and May Dugger home left background. (Courtesy: Anna Dugger Adkins)

Butler, Watauga Academy, 1946: Asa Stout, Jr. and R.G. Perkins, Jr. (Courtesy: Leta Grindstaff Lewis)

**Midway 1952: Eli Finley Tester (1872-1954) and Jessie 'Ad 'Kimberlin (1882-1963)
(Compiler Photo)**

Roan Valley, 1925: Oscar Fritts and Dexter Stevens (Courtesy: Nancy Fritts Tester)

Grandfather Mountain, 1936 Tester Reunion: Clockwise from right: E.F. Tester, Camoline Presnell Tester, Harvey Tester, Charlene Tester, Louis Tester, Howard Tester, Carroll Tester, Mary Jo Main, Nettie Cable Main, Coy Rominger, Stella Main, Earl Tester, Pierce Tester, Park Main, Ben Tester, Loudell Tew Tester, Herman Tester, Luke Tester, Dee Cable Tester, Mae Tester, Ida Tester Finney, Billy Finney.
(Courtesy: Dee Tester)

Alice Wagner Jewett   Roan Valley 1930:   Lillie Wagner
(All Photos Courtesy: Bobby Wagner)

Roan Valley 1920's:
l-r Tessie Moreland, Tishie Wagner, Bonnie Moreland

**Roan Valley, 1945: Daniel Wilbur Wagner (1910-1963)
Interred in the Wagner Cemetery, Lakeview Drive, Watauga Lake (Courtesy: Bobby Wagner)**

Roan Valley, Mill Creek, 1920's: Alma Ward and Hazel Ward and Toby
(All Photos Courtesy: Alma Ward Worley)

Lt. Stephen Brown (1843-1912) {wife Addie Wagner} and Capt. Barton Roby Brown (1841-1928) {wife Callie Wagner} Confederate States of America. All are interred in the Wagner Cemetery, Mount Farm, Maymead.

Carl Hollaway (Courtesy: Linda Tester Hollaway)

Elk Valley, Sugar Hollow 1945: Eli Finley Tester (Courtesy: Juanita Tester Wilson)

Etta Crosswhite Griffey (1890-1967) (Courtesy: Bobby Wagner)

Roan Valley, 1928: Georgia Church and Pansy Grindstaff (Courtesy: Margaret Cress)

Roan Valley, 1942: Esma Proffitt, Pansy (Pat) Stout, Lowell Stout, Eula Stout (Courtesy: Bobby Wagner)

Roan Valley, Mill Creek, 1910's: l-r 1st row: Eula Church, Georgia Church, John Church, Ruby Pleasant, Walter Pleasant, Sanna Church Pleasant, Laura Pleasant, l-r back row: Thelma Church, Grace Church
(Courtesy: Margaret Cress)

Elbert McCloud   (Courtesy: Anna Ruth Rush)   James (Soup) McCloud

Dryden McCloud (Courtesy: Anna Ruth Rush)

George and Rachel Atwood (Courtesy: Mary Walker Ward)

**Dry Hill, 1940's: l-r Haskel Griffey, Joe Leonard, Parker Stout, D. L. Stansberry
(Courtesy: Bobby Wagner)**

**Alice Grindstaff Wagner (1879-1915) and Elbert Wagner (1879-1940)
Interred in the Wagner Cemetery, Watauga Lake (Courtesy: Bobby Wagner)**

**Watauga Valley, 1935: Frank, Scott, Fayette, William and Joe Burton
(Courtesy: Florence Tucker)**

Watauga Valley, 1904: sitting l-r Frank Burton, John R. Stansberry; standing l-r Matilda Burton Tucker, Avery Miller, Mary Burton Miller, Ella Burton Bunton, Cora Burton
(Courtesy: Linda Tucker Jewett)

Frank Jewett, Dry Hill, served the United States in both World War I and World War II. He is interred with his wife, Chloe Blackburn Jewett, in the Rock Springs Church Cemetery, Watauga Lake.
(Courtesy: Linda Tucker Jewett)

Frank (Buster) Jewett, son of Chloe Blackburn Jewett and Frank Jewett (Courtesy: Linda Tucker Jewett)

Frank Jewett, Jr. son of Frank, Sr. (Buster) Jewett and Linda Tucker Jewett
(Courtesy: Linda Tucker Jewett)

Watauga Valley, Sugar Grove 1900: Seated are the youngest living three of the '20' Duggers, l-r Emily Dugger Bunton (1830-1912), Soloman Quince Dugger (1828-1910)and Nancy Dugger Anderson (1825-1919) Mrs. Bunton is interred in the Buntontown Cemetery, Mrs. Anderson in the Cowan Cemetery, Cowantown and Mr. Dugger in the Julius Dugger Cemetery, Sugar Grove. The youngest of the '20' Duggers was Mildred Dugger Anderson (1833-1871). She is interred in the Julius Dugger Cemetery. Standing are Rebecca Bunton and Katie Whitehead (Courtesy: Juanita Tester Wilson)

Cowantown, Burton Family Reunion 1953: L side of table, 1st row: Frances Dugger (hands over face) Mary Burton Miller, Matilda Burton Tucker, Joe Bunton (beside his wife Ella Burton Bunton), Louise Tucker Pleasant beside Ruth Burton Moody, Frances Swift Bunton holding Scottie Jack beside Scott Bunton, Troy Stansberry, Fred McGuire, Elbert Tucker. L side 2nd row: Rose Burton McGuire, Lucretia Forrester Dugger, William Burton, Lucinda Isaacs Burton. R side of table, 1st row: Linda Pleasant, Debbie Miller, Trula Pleasant, Barbara Dugger (part face showing), Cora Burton, Eileen McGuire (to left of Cora), Elma Ruth Bunton, Helen Dugger (left of Elma Ruth), Martha Burton Taylor, Kyle Stansberry (right of Martha), Paul Stansberry (in front of his mother, Millicent Burton Stansberry, Ellis Tucker (behind Ellis is George Smotherman), In front of Ellis is Sam Moody, behind Sam is Celia Stansberry Dugger and Frank Miller. R side 2nd row: Richard Miller, Lafayette Burton, Grant Reece, Millard Scott Burton, Joe Burton, Florence Tucker holding Mike Pleasant, Karl Pleasant. R side 3rd row: Rebecca Bunton Burton, Crate Blevins, Bobby Stansberry, Norman Stansberry, Stella Reece Burton and Raleigh Burton. (All Photos Courtesy: Martha Bunton Query)

Cowantown, 1950: Scott Burton Farm

Alma Ward (Courtesy: Alma Ward Worley)

Lena Forrester, Dexter Forrester (All Photos Courtesy: Juanita Tester Wilson)

Midway, 1956: Clockwise from left: Steve Tester, Toot Ward, Buster Jewett, Larry Bradley, Luke Tester, Bill Fletcher, Doug Bradley, Powell Wilson

Midway 1930's: Arthur Irick (Courtesy: Juanita Tester Wilson)

**World War I: Arthur Cable and Hopson Millsaps
(Courtesy: Juanita Tester Wilson))**

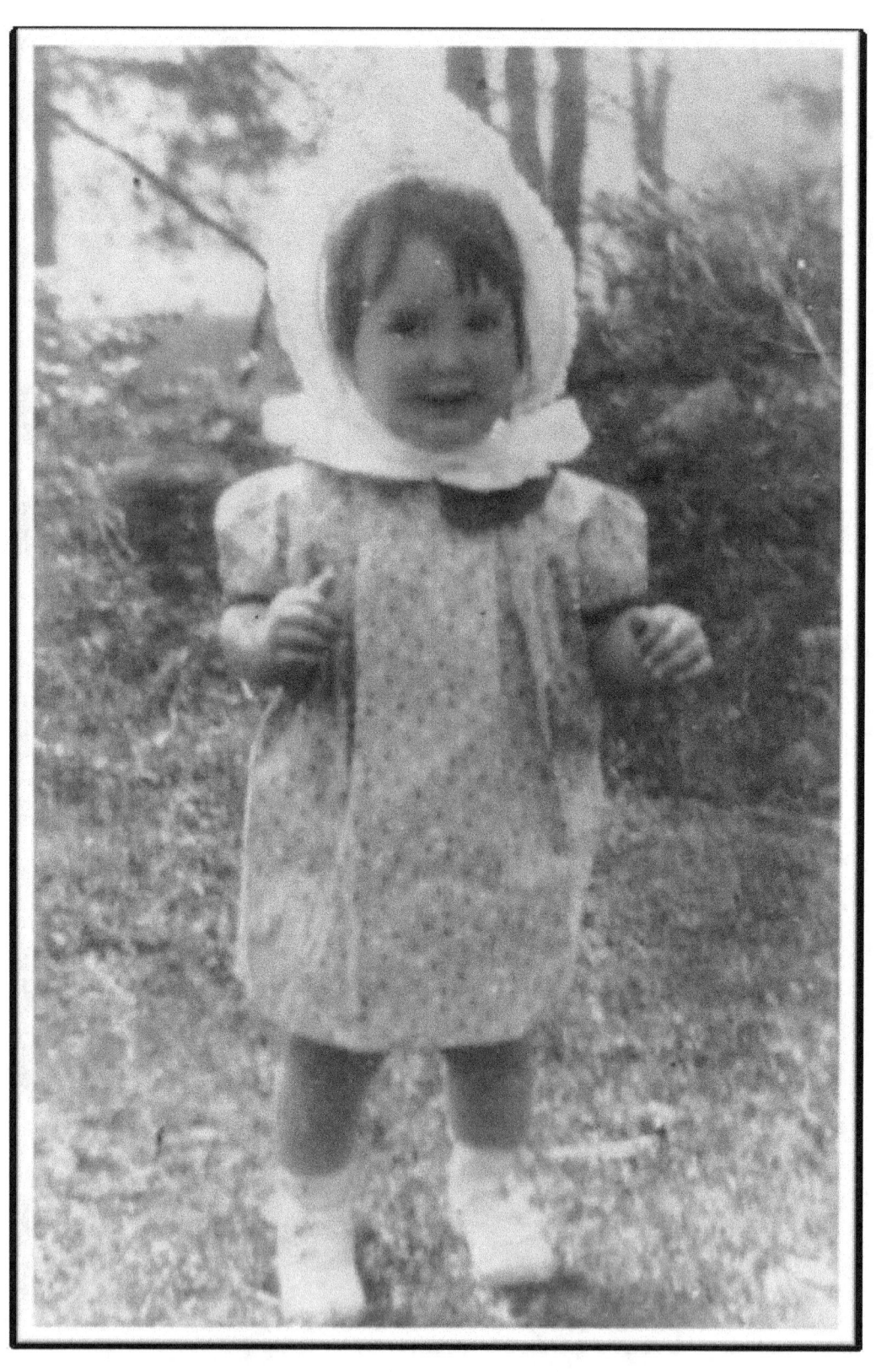

Carolyn Tester (Courtesy: Juanita Tester Wilson)

**Cobb Creek 1942: Bob Matheson and Verdie Slemp Matheson
(Courtesy: Bobby Wagner)**

**Lynch, Kentucky, International Harvester Company Store 1930: Bob Fritts, right,
(Courtesy: Nancy Fritts Tester)**

**Buntontown 1920's: Avery Harmon (1893-1980) and Annie Mae Bunton Harmon (1899-1970)
Interred in the Buntontown Cemetery (Courtesy: Mary Walker Ward)**

Sallie Hately (Courtesy: Mary Walker Ward)

**Backbone Rock 1950's: Carolyn Tester and Eleanor Kimberlin
(Courtesy: Juanita Tester Wilson)**

1919: Curtis Forrester, Della Forrester, Ross Forrester (Courtesy: Juanita Tester Wilson)

**Dry Hill, 1946: l-r: Chalmas Laws, McKinley Laws, Mack Hollaway and Gordon Garland
(Courtesy: Linda Tester Hollaway)**

Watauga Valley, Cowantown 1941: Haynes Dugger (Courtesy: Haynes Dugger)

Haynes Dugger (Courtesy: Haynes Dugger)

Douglas Alan Dugger (Courtesy: Haynes Dugger)

**Dry Hill, 1925: McKinley Laws and Ethel Greenwell Laws and children, Chalmas and Marie
(Courtesy: Juanita Tester Wilson)**

**Midway, 1958: Carolyn Tester; Sink Mountain and Watauga Lake in background
(Courtesy: Juanita Tester Wilson)**

Roan Valley, Midway W. T. Bradley Farm "Over on the Hill" 1920's:
Ketha (Goose) Bradley, Norvan (Nub) Bradley
(Courtesy: Juanita Tester Wilson)

Roan Valley, 1940's: Charles Dugger (Courtesy: Anna Dugger Adkins)

**Watauga River, Sugar Grove 1950: John Cable (1858-1953) with wife Jane Greenwell Cable (1861-1929) interred in the Cable Cemetery, Sugar Grove, Watauga Lake.
(Courtesy: Juanita Tester Wilson)**

1945: Mary Lorene Forrester and Frances Charlene Tester
(Courtesy: Juanita Tester Wilson)

Midway, Cardwell Home, 1950's: Novalee Grindstaff Cardwell and Dee Cable Tester

Watauga Lake 1960's: Steve Tester (All Photos Courtesy: Juanita Tester Wilson)

Roan Valley 1950's: 'Neice' Forrester Holloway (Bob Holloway with fish)

Midway 1950's: Bruce Reed (All Photos Courtesy: Juanita Tester Wilson)

**Roan Valley, Butler, Benjamin and Sara Stevens home 1941: Jimmy Kimberlin and Eleanor Kimberlin
(Courtesy: Juanita Tester Wilson)**

Roan Valley, 1940's: Jewell Grindstaff

Roan Valley, Old Little Dry Run Road, 1940's: Dora Grindstaff
(All Photos Courtesy: Juanita Tester Wilson)

Roan Valley, Midway, 1940: Leta Grindstaff, Lena Forrester, Rosalie Bradley
(Courtesy: Juanita Tester Wilson)

**Daniel J. Grindstaff (1892-1956) and Ada Proffitt Grindstaff (1896-1986) are interred in the Rock Springs Baptist Church Cemetery, Watauga Lake.
(All Photos Courtesy: Juanita Tester Wilson)**

Roan Valley, Old Little Dry Run Road 1945: l-r sisters, Myrtle Grindstaff Forrester, Lena Grindstaff Garland, Leta Grindstaff Lewis (Courtesy: Juanita Tester Wilson)

Roan Valley, 1942: Leta Grindstaff, (Courtesy: Juanita Tester Wilson)

Midway, 1950's: Ketha Bradley and Zola Bradley with children, Rose Mary and Charles

1940's: Jay Depew and Mary O'Dell Blackburn (All Photos Courtesy: Juanita Tester Wilson)

**Watauga Lake, 1950's: l-r Powell Wilson, Bruce Reed, Toot Ward, Buster Jewett, Jess Wagner
(All Photos Courtesy: Juanita Tester Wilson)**

**Dry Hill, 1950's: Roscoe Forrester (1883- 1974) and Jo Ann Wolfe Forrester (1890-1976)
Interred in the Dry Hill Cemetery above their former home**

Roan Valley, Southern Railroad Tracks 1940: Leta Grindstaff and Lena Grindstaff
(Courtesy: Juanita Tester Wilson)

Little Dry Run Road, Midway School Water Pump, Midway Church, Hill & Pearl Blackburn Home in background. 1940's: Herbert Lewis and Leta Grindstaff Lewis. (Courtesy: Juanita Tester Wilson)

**Watauga Lake, Little Dry Run Branch, 1951: Jimmy Kimberlin and Bobby Wagner
(Courtesy: Juanita Tester Wilson)**

Zola Kimberlin Bradley and Ketha (Goose) Bradley with sons, baby Charles and Jack Cable (Courtesy: Juanita Tester Wilson)

Mr. Curtis Forrester (Courtesy: Juanita Tester Wilson)

Children of Samuel J. Forrester and Amanda McElyea Forrester. Clockwise from left: Della b. 1889, Polly Anna b. 1897, Wm. Elbert {Doc} b. 1894, Lulu Jean b. 1891, Harriet Lucetia b. 1882, Roscoe {R.R.} b. 1883, Barcia Lona b. 1885, Bertie b. 1887. (All Photos Courtesy: Juanita Tester Wilson)

Amanda McElyea Tester Forrester (1853-1938) and Samuel J. Forrester (1852-1941) Interred in the Bradley Cemetery, Midway, Watauga Lake

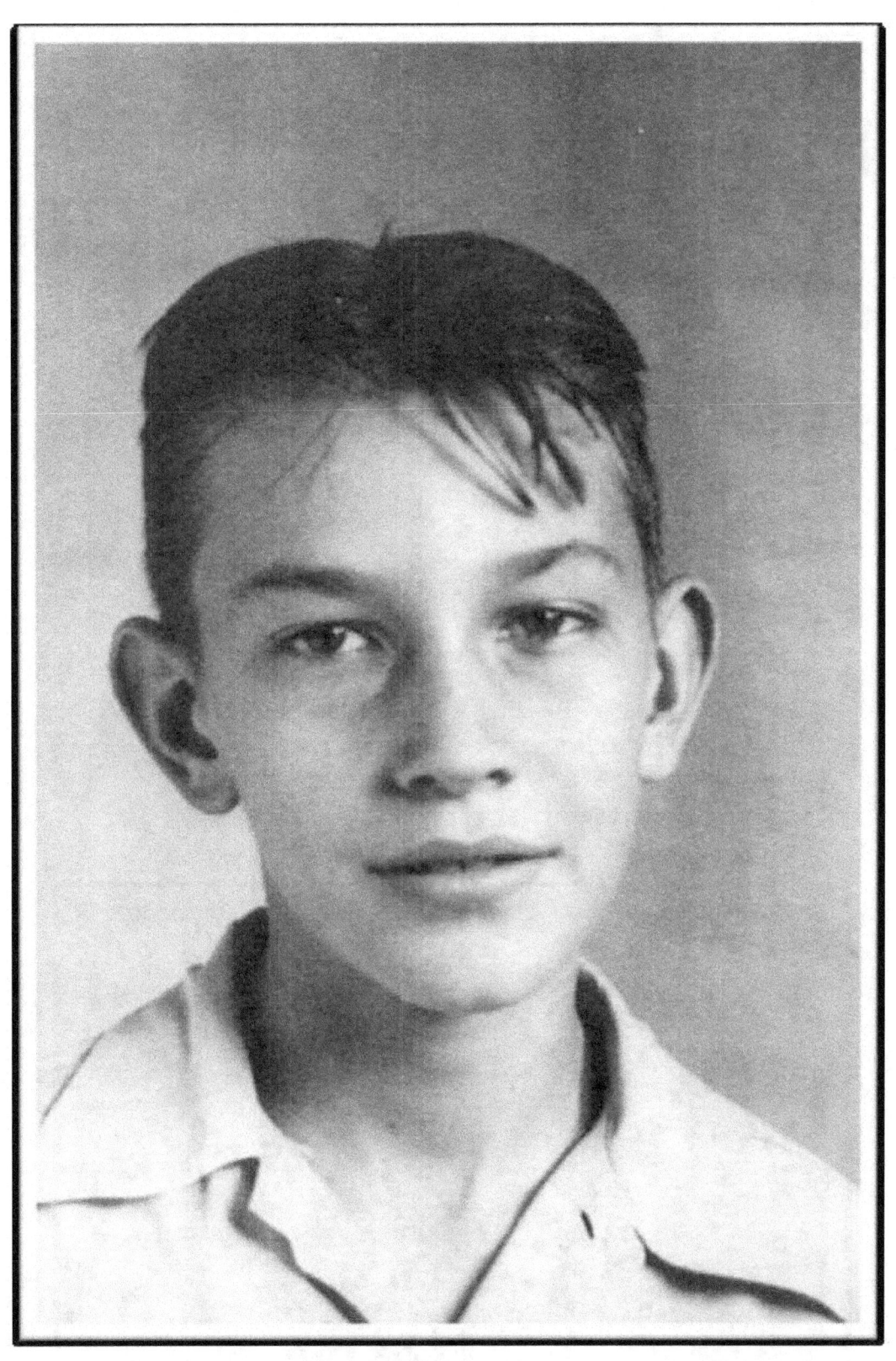

James Barton Forrester (1939-1959) Son of Wm. Elbert (Doc) Forrester and Texa Greenwell Forrester. Brother to Lorene, Lena and Dexter. Interred in the Dry Hill Cemetery. (Courtesy: Juanita Tester Wilson)

Midway, 1954: l-r Juanita Tester, Ronald (Bud) Wagner, Carroll Fletcher

Little Dry Run Road, Midway School Grounds, 1942: Lena Grindstaff, Lena Forrester, Mary Odell Blackburn, Leta Grindstaff, Rosalie Bradley (All Photos Courtesy: Juanita Tester Wilson)

Midway, Christman 1938: Howard Trivette and Herman Tester
(Courtesy: Juanita Tester Wilson)

Little Dry Run, Kimberlin Farm 1950's:
Front: Jimmy, Keith, Clifford; Back: Jeanette and Maude (Courtesy: Juanita Tester Wilson)

Watauga Valley 1920's: William Elbert (Doc) Forrester and Texa Greenwell Forrester
(Courtesy: Juanita Tester Wilson)

**Johnson County High School, 1950's: Archie Dean Stout and Emma Lou Bradley
(Courtesy: Juanita Tester Wilson)**

Roan Creek Bridge at Bob Grindstaff's Store 1940,: Leta Grindstaff and Herbert Lewis
(All Photos Courtesy: Juanita Tester Wilson)

Watauga River Bridge, Butler 1940:
Carl Stanton, Leta Grindstaff Earl Stanton, Lena Forrest

1941 Roan Creek Bridge at Bob Grindstaff's Store, Earl Stanton and Mae Tester
(All Photos Courtesy: Juanita Tester Wilson)

Roan Creek Southern RR Trestle (1st above Butler) 1941: T.J. Grindstaff and Lena Forrester

WW I:

William Elbert (Doc) Forrester

Watauga Valley, Big Dry Run, 1927: l-r Samuel Forrester, Amanda Forrester, Texa Forrester holding Dexter, Lou Hollaway, Austin Hollaway, in front Elbert and Lena. (All Photos Courtesy: Juanita Tester Wilson)

Chalmas Laws (Courtesy: Juanita Tester Wilson)

Roan Valley, The Rufus Hollow, 1927: l-r Tommy Grindstaff, Leta Grindstaff, Lena Grindstaff, Myrtle Grindstaff (All Photos Courtesy: Juanita Tester Wilson)

The Kimberlin Family: l-r Ralph, Jessie (Ad), Lena Mae, Zola, Sarah (Ettie), Clifford

**Lucus N. and Thelma Church Cress Home, Mill Creek, Neva, 1940:
l-r Jack Cress, Barbara Ward, Joe Mack Cress. (All Photos Courtesy: Margaret Cress)**

**Isaac Lafayette Wagner (1858-1935) and Nancy Naomi Wagner (1861-1933).
Interred in the Wagner Cemetery, Lakeview Drive, Watauga Lake**

Butler, Watauga Bridge 1945: Florence Tucker and Emily Grindstaff
(Courtesy: Mary Walker Ward)

**Roan Valley, Old Roan Creek Road at Old Little Dry Run Road, Bob Grindstaff Store 1940's:
l-r Leon Ward, Frances Laws, Carl Stanton, Irene Laws (Courtesy: Juanita Tester Wilson)**

Truman Dugger
(Courtesy: Hazel Dugger Pierce)

Louise Hackney
(Courtesy: Claude Matheson)

Dr. Ira M. Gambill
(Courtesy: Billy Joe Milhorn)

Watauga Valley, Sugar Grove 1904: Family of Benjamin D. Cable and Susannah Simerly Cable.
Sitting: John Cable and William Cable. Standing l-r Susie Cable, Levicy Cable Smith, Benjamin D. Cable,
Susannah Simerly Cable, Celia Simerly McKinney, Mary Cable Baker, Rebecca Cable Dugger
(All Photos Courtesy: Juanita Tester Wilson)

Mary Cable Baker and
David Baker

Doeville 1950's: Dewey Cable (1899-1968) and Josie Laws Cable (1902-1974) and sons, Richard and Frank. Mr. and Mrs. Cable are interred in the Cable Cemetery, Sugar Grove, Watauga Lake.
(Courtesy: Juanita Tester Wilson)

1961: Frank Cable (Compiler Photo)

Elk Valley, Sugar Hollow 1920's: Sarah Camoline Presnell Tester (1880-1947)
(Courtesy: Juanita Tester Wilson)

**Watauga Valley, Sugar Grove 1918: Nettie Cable with her twin sisters Alta and Alma Cable
(Courtesy: Juanita Tester Wilson)**

Watauga Valley, Sugar Grove 1920's: Ella Anderson Cable (1876-1940)
(Courtesy: Juanita Tester Wilson)

Elk River Valley 1920's: Parker Main Sr. and Nettie Cable Main.
Interred in the Whitehead Cemetery, Lower Elk, Watauga Lake
(Courtesy: Juanita Tester Wilson)

Elk Valley, Sugar Hollow, The Tester Family 1924:
seated Eli Finley Tester with Ruth Tester, Camoline Presnell Tester holding Mae Tester.
standing l-r 1st row Luke Tester, Louis Tester, Nelson Tester, Ruby Tester
.l-r 2nd row Rilda Tester Campbell holding Lena Campbell, Ida Tester Finney, Aner Tester Rominger, Ben Tester. l-r 3rd row Dewey Campbell, Pierce Tester, Earl Tester, Coy Rominger, Coy Tester.
(Courtesy: Juanita Tester Wilson)

**Elk Valley, Little Milligan 1950's: Park Main, Sr. and Nettie Cable Main.
(Compiler Photo)**

Jaunita Tester Greenwell and R.H. Greenwell (Courtesy: Dan Stansberry)

Sugar Grove 1920s: l-r Frank Dugger, Vertie Green Dugger, Martha Gregg, Vertie Cable, Minnie Miller, Dewey Cable, Rilda Green Cable (Courtesy: Juanita Tester Wilson)

Elk Valley, Sugar Hollow 1942: l-r Billy Finney, Herman Tester, Billy Luther
(Courtesy: Juanita Tester Wilson)

Watauga Valley 1920: Ezra Oliver Anderson (1855-1926) and Nancy Caroline Clawson Anderson (1854-1925) Interred in the Sugar Grove Baptist Church Cemetery, Watauga Lake.
(All Photos Courtesy: Juanita Tester Wilson)

Joseph Oliver Dugger (1856-1945) and Rebecca Cable Dugger (1865-1922)

Midway 1937: Dee Tester holding Juanita Tester

Midway 1941: Juanita Tester
(All Photos Courtesy: Juanita Tester Wilson)

Midway 1939: Juanita Tester

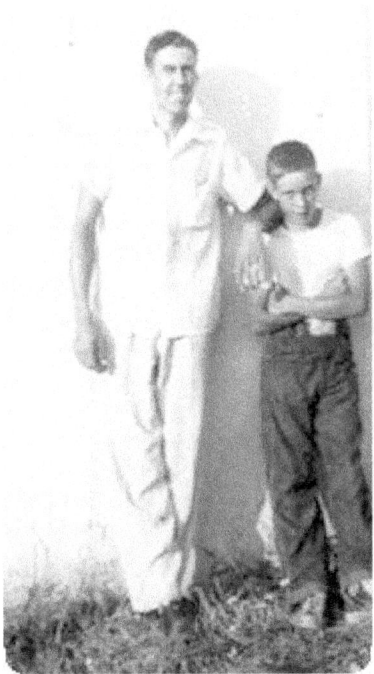  

Roan Creek Dock 1952: Jack Wilson Jr. and Powell Wilson

Jack Wilson Jr.

Jack Wilson Jr. holding Mike Wilson

Watauga Lake, Kyte Hollow 1962: l-r Jack Wilson Sr., Joda Johnson Wilson, Celestine Wilson, Doyle Wilson Jack Wilson Jr., Veril Wilson, Powell Wilson (All Photos Courtesy: Juanita Tester Wilson)

Watauga Lake, Roan Creek Restaurant 1950's: Bob Holloway and Jack Wilson Jr.

**Watauga Lake, Roan Valley, Roan Creek Dock 1959:
Jack Wilson, Sr. and state record Rainbow Trout (Courtesy: Juanita Tester Wilson)**

Sugar Hollow, Tester Reunion, 1941: l-r Alta Bunton Tester,
Ben Tester, Eugene Jones Sr. and Dee Tester

Sugar Hollow, Tester Reunion, 1941: Eugene Jones, Sr. and Luke Tester
(All Photos Courtesy: Juanita Tester Wilson)

Sugar Hollow 1940's: Ruby Tester Trivette, Ruth Tester Jones, Mae Tester Cook

Sugar Hollow 1924: l-r Lewis Tester, Ruby Tester and Ruth Tester
(All Photos Courtesy: Juanita Tester Wilson)

**Elk Valley, Sugar Hollow 1936: Charlene Tester, Dee Tester, Herman Tester and Luke Tester
(Courtesy: Juanita Tester Wilson)**

Cosby 1930's: Dewey Campbell and Rilda Tester Campbell and children, Clay, Claude, Charlie, Carl and Lena (All Photos Courtesy: Juanita Tester Wilson)

Watauga Valley, Sugar Grove 1935: Dewey Cable

Steven Kent Tester (Compiler Photo)

Baker Gap 1920's: Peter Lee Lyons (1874-1933) and Martha Nichols Lyons (1877-1933) and eight of their ten children. Their children were George, Sam, Dewey, Robert, Carl, Jack, Lenore, Ethel, Beulah and Maude. Mr. Lyons was the pastor of Mountain View Baptist Church when it was moved and renamed Bakers Gap Baptist Church. He and Mrs. Lyons were killed in a collision with a train in Elizabethton at the Keenburg crossing in 1933.
(Courtesy: Juanita Tester Wilson)

Roan Valley, Stout Branch 1945: Robert (Bob) and Sallie Matheson Fritts family l-r Bob, Dwight, Jim, Sallie holding Betty, Nancy, Harold and Lois (Courtesy: Nancy Fritts Tester)

Roland Elac Tester and Hound Dog (Courtesy: Nancy Fritts Tester)

Roan Valley, Rufus Hollow 1934: Mrs. Ettie Proffitt Kimberlin holds their son, Clyde and Mr. Ad Kimberlin holds their grandson, Jack Cable
(Courtesy: Juanita Tester Wilson)

Midway 1950's: Lena Mae Kimberlin Bradley holding Norma Jean, Larry Bradley on left and Dennis Bradley on right (Courtesy: Juanita Tester Wilson)

**Roan Valley, Old Roan Creek Road 1940: Luke Tester
(Courtesy: Juanita Tester Wilson)**

William Elbert (Doc) Forrester (Courtesy: Juanita Tester Wilson)

**D. L. Stansberry
(Courtesy: Dan Stansberry)**

Sugar Grove, Cable Reunion 1947:
Front l-r Luke Tester, Mary Jo Main, Nettie Main, Juanita Tester, Pat Tester, Carolyn Tester, Richard Cable, Frank Cable, Josie Cable holding Larry Cable (All Photos Courtesy: Juanita Tester Wilson)

Watauga Valley, Sugar Grove 1924:
William Cable (1869-1930) and Ella Anderson Cable (1876-1940) and family
l-r William, Ella, Nettie, Dewey, Annie, Ordie, Verdie Delores, Alma and Alta

Watauga Valley 1890's:
Thomas B. Anderson (1857-1944)
Amanda Dugger Anderson (1860-1925)
Mr. Anderson is interred in the Sugar Grove Church Cemetery; Mrs. Anderson is interred in the Dugger Cemetery at Sugar Grove.

'Uncle' John Cable (1858-1953) and Jane Greenwell Cable (1861-1929) are interred in the Sugar Grove Church Cemetery, Watauga Lake. (All Photos Courtesy: Juanita Tester Wilson)

Roan Valley, Bee Hollow 1900: l-r front Andrew Jackson Fritts (1836-1917) and Louisa Porch Fritts (1840-1915), James F. Smith holding Mary, Martha Fritts Smith, l-r back John Fritts, Wilburn Fritts, Matilda Fritts, Elizabeth Smith and Brownlow Fritts. Mr. and Mrs. Fritts are interred in the Fritts Cemetery, Bee Hollow, Watauga Lake on property they once owned. (Courtesy: Una Fritts Glick)

Fate Morley (Courtesy: Peart Morley Matherly)

Wilma Dugger and Anna Dugger (Courtesy: Anna Dugger Adkins)

Midway School, Little Dry Run Road 1942: l-r Elmer Blackburn, Herman Tester, Leo Arnold, Howard Jewett, Howard Cable, John Forrester (Courtesy: Hazel Dugger Pierce)

Thelma Church Cress (1904-1976) interred in Brown Cemetery, Pine Grove with husband Lucas N. (Bud) Cress (1895-1963) (Courtesy: Margaret Cress)

Midway School, Little Dry Run Road 1942: from left 1st row Colleen Arnold, Vadie Laws, Elsie Grindstaff, Hazel Dugger, 2nd row Charlene Tester, Lorene Forrester, 3rd row Mary Lou Grindstaff, Evadna Proffitt, Virginia Lee South, Rosalie Laws, 4th row Edward Grindstaff, Justin Grindstaff, Jim Cable, Clyde Fenner, Jr. (Courtesy: Hazel Dugger Pierce)

Midway School, Little Dry Run Road 1942: Photograph includes Rondal (Bud) Wagner, Elmer Blackburn, Daryl Keller, Howard (Toot) Jewett, Roger Pierce, Bobby Jack Ward, Howard Cable, John (Beet) Forrester, Dorothy Fletcher, Anna Ruth Blackburn, J. D. Slemp, Shirley Wagner, Herman Tester, Ilean Grindstaff, Emma Ruth Forrester and others (Courtesy: Hazel Dugger Pierce)

**Butler 1930's: l-r Ellard (Birdeye) Millsaps and Dr. Ira Gambill
(Courtesy: Mary Walker Ward)**

Carl Matherly (Courtesy: Mary Walker Ward)   Floyd Bradley (Courtesy: Joyce Dean Garrison)

Roan Valley, Butler 1940's: Anna Reece Cable and Terry Millsaps (Courtesy: Florence Tucker)

World War II: Ernest Snyder (Courtesy: Mary Walker Ward)

Roan Valley, Rock Springs 1934: l-r Nell Fritts, Elsie Fritts holding Wiley Fritts, Violet Fritts
(Courtesy: Nancy Fritts Tester)

Butler 1930's: Bess Crosswhite Swift (All Photos Courtesy: Florence Tucker)

Butler 1930's: Bill Trivette carrying Anna Trivette

Roan Valley, Fritts Curve 1935: Donald Lunceford
(Courtesy: Una Fritts Glick)

**Roan Valley, Neva 1920's: Firefighting Committee, Wiley Fritts 1st left, Brady Fritts 3rd from right
(Courtesy: Una Fritts Glick)**

Cobb Creek 1942: Avery Matheson, Ora Matheson, Luther Matheson (Courtesy: Barbara Henley Styles)

**1940's: Ray Trivette and George Walker
(Courtesy: George Walker)**

**Roan Valley, Neva, Pine Grove, 1924: Barton Roby Brown (center front with bowtie) and family
(Courtesy: Louise McQueen Shull)**

1905: l-r Nell Davis (Mrs. Wiley Ward) and Maude Davis (Mrs. Charles Ward), daughters of Robert Daniel Davis (1861-1940) and Ella Hawkins Davis (1865-1937) Mr. and Mrs. Davis are interred in the Hawkins Cemetery in Crackers Neck, Neva. (Courtesy: Alma Ward Worley)

WW II: French Neatherly
(Courtesy: French Neatherly)

Butler, Watauga Academy 1930's: Mr. Homer Farthing
(Courtesy: Mary Walker Ward)

Callona Cress (1868-1940)

Mr. and Mrs. Cress are interred in the Brown Cemetery, Pine Grove, Neva.
(All Photos Courtesy: Margaret Cress)

Robert L. Cress (1869-1930)

Watauga River, Sugar Grove 1944: l-r back Luke Tester, Nell Baker, Isaac Cable, front Herman Tester (Courtesy: Juanita Tester Wilson)

Butler, 1941: Ed Hyder, Lucille McQueen, Janet Greenwell, Peggy Laws, Otis Ward, Ethel Slemp (Courtesy: Mary Walker Ward)

Stout Branch, Neva 1927: Rachel Bailey Matheson (1844-1928) interred in the Matheson-Stout Cemetery, Stout Branch. She and Henry Harold Matheson (1841-1901) interred in the Grassy Valley Cemetery, Knoxville, were the parents of four children: Frances (Lum), Carley, Robert (Bob) and John Henry Matheson (Courtesy: Nancy Fritts Tester)

**Watauga Academy Faculty 1945: Mr. George Jenkins, Mrs. Alma Worley, Miss Betty Early, Mr. Mark Reece
(Courtesy: Florence Tucker)**

**John E. Dugger (1857-1930) reinterred with wife Martha Greenwell Dugger (1861-1925) in Butler Memorial Cemetery, Butler. Watauga Lake required removal from the Rainbolt Cemetery, Old Butler.
(Courtesy: George Walker)**

WW II: Howard Bradley (Courtesy: Margie Bradley)

Butler Springs, Old Watauga River Road 1947: Lorraine Millsaps (Courtesy: Florence Tucker)

WW II: Clarence Ward (Courtesy: Jewel Dean Ward McCloud)

Lee Cable (Courtesy: Tammy Wilson Paul)

Clifford Kimberlin and Maude Stevens Kimberlin (Courtesy: Juanita Wilson Tester)

Watauga Valley, Banner Elk NC 1915: Nettie Cable and Lou Cable (Courtesy: Juanita Tester Wilson)

Elk Valley, Lower Elk, 1942: Mary Jo Main, Herman Tester, Juanita Tester (Compiler Photo)

WWII: Otis Ward
(Courtesy: Jewel Dean Ward McCloud

WW II.: Smith Weaver
(Courtesy: Mary Walker Ward

Butler, Watauga Academy 1931: Maude Gregg (1911-2010)
(Courtesy: Florence Tucker))

**Hopper Creek, Doe Mountain, Neva 1928: Wiley Fritts
(Courtesy: Una Fritts Glick)**

Mrs. Bess DeVault (Courtesy: Florence Tucker)

Selma (Babe) Curtis (Courtesy: Florence Tucker)

Midway Service Station and Grocery, 1950: Neta Bradley (1897-1977).
Interred in the Bradley Cemetery, Midway, Watauga Lake.

Elk Valley 1940's: front W. K. Main, Stacy Main, Park Main; back Hattie Lewis, Sallie Miller, Eula Isaacs, Lara Lunceford (All Photos Courtesy: Juanita Tester Wilson)

Watauga Valley, 1910's: John E. Dugger (Courtesy: George Walker)

Robert M. DeVault Sr.
(Courtesy: Florence Tucker)

**Butler 1930's: Doris and Dorothy DeVault
(Courtesy: Florence Tucker)**

**Butler, 1930: l-r Edwin, Leonard, Doris, Dorothy and Robert M. DeVault Jr.
(All Photos Courtesy: Florence Tucker)**

Robert M. DeVault, Jr.

Dry Hill, McKinley and Ethel Greenwell Laws home 1930's: Chalmas Laws
(Courtesy: Juanita Tester Wilson)

**Carl Blackburn and wife; later in WW II. Carl was the most decorated soldier from Johnson County
(Compiler Photo)**

Midway 1953: Steve Tester and Pat Tester
(All Photos Courtesy: Juanita Tester Wilson)

Midway 1938: Herman Tester and Juanita Tester

A. B. (Bert) Greenwell (1832-1909) and Mary Cable Greenwell (1830-1919) lived in the Roan Valley, Dry Hill., Duncan Hollow. They are interred in the Greenwell Cemetery, Duncan Hollow, Watauga Lake located on land which they once owned. (Compiler Photo)

Raleigh Matheson
(Courtesy: Nancy Fritts Tester)

Watauga Valley, Sugar Grove, 1940: Ordie Cable Potter at kitchen entrance to her home place the William and Ella Cable home, .Log home was built by Benjamin C. Cable in the 1820's and served as home to three generations and their families: Benjamin C. and wife Rebecca and family; Benjamin D. and wife Susanna and family and William and wife Ella and family . In 1947 this revered old house was razed and burned by the TVA to clear the land of buildings for the Watauga Project and subsequently the Watauga Dam and Lake. This home site and most of 'Cable Valley' is now deep under water. (Courtesy: Juanita Tester Wilson)

Hopper Creek, Doe Mountain, Neva 1920: Nettie Lunceford Fritts (1878-1955) (Courtesy: Una Fritts Glick)

Watauga Valley, Sugar Grove 1920's: John Potter holding Bernice (Essie), Ordie Cable Potter and Harold (Courtesy: Juanita Tester Wilson)

Matheson Farm, Stout Branch, Neva 1941: John Henry Matheson (1875-1968) and Catherine Stout Matheson (1877-1956) (Courtesy: Nancy Fritts Tester)

John Fritts
(Courtesy: Una Fritts Glick)

Midway 1954: Steve Tester (Courtesy: Dee Tester)

Warren Tucker (Courtesy: Linda Tucker Jewett)

**Ash Trail Service Station and Garage, Hampton 1930's: Troy Tucker on right.
(Courtesy: Louise Tucker Pleasant)**

Mary Ramsey (Courtesy: Florence Tucker)

William and Annie Sevier (Courtesy: Shirley Glenn Stout)

**Vestal Ray Cowan (1932-1951) Killed in Korea, interred in the Buntontown Cemetery.
(Compiler Photo)**

Watauga Valley 1930's: Rosa and Dove BurtonAsa Bunton
(All Photos Courtesy: Martha Bunton Query)

Raymond Bunton

Joseph Scott Bunton (1926-1980) interred in the Sugar Grove Baptist Church Cemetery, Sugar Grove, Watauga Lake (Courtesy: Martha Bunton Query)

Martha Belle Bunton (Courtesy: Martha Bunton Query)

Butler, 1930's: Carson Whitehead (Courtesy: Sara Whitehead Sellers)

Watauga Valley, Spring Branch Hollow 1940's: Lucky Dugger (1925-1967) interred in the Sugar Grove Baptist Church Cemetery, Sugar Grove, Watauga Lake (Courtesy: Hazel Dugger Pierce)

Butler, Watauga River Bridge 1940's: R.L. Arney and D. G. Stout (Courtesy: Mary Walker Ward)

WW II:
Fleenor Stout

WW II:
Lacy Stout

(All Photos Courtesy: Joyce Dean Stout Garrison)

**World War II: D. G. Stout
(Courtesy: Joyce Dean Stout)**

Frank Conrad Bunton (1905-1936) and Gladys Pearl Burton Bunton ((1910-1956) are interred in the Sugar Grove Baptist Church Cemetery, Sugar Grove, Watauga Lake.
Mr. Bunton was killed while performing his duty as a law enforcement officer in Butler.

U. S. Grant Bunton and Martha Bunton
(All Photos Courtesy: Martha Bunton Query)

Elk Valley, Sugar Hollow 1920's: Back: Rilda Tester Campbell and Lena Campbell, Martha Tester Heaton, E.F. Tester, Camoline Presnell Tester, Ida Tester Finney, Mid: Ruby Tester, Ruth Tester, Susan Presnell, Mae Tester, Front: Howard Tester, Bonnie Finney (Courtesy: Juanite Tester Wilson)

**Roan Valley, Glenn and Leona Dugger Walker Home 1940's:
l-r Edna Hyder, Emily Grindstaff, Mary Walker
(All Photos Courtesy: Mary Walker Ward)**

Watauga Academy 1940's: Teacher Mark Reece and Frank Jenkins

**Elk Valley, Shell Creek 1930's: Jack Sr. and Joda Johnson Wilson Family
front l-r Doyle, Veril, Jack Jr. back l-r Jack Sr. Joda and Celestine
(Courtesy: Juanita Tester Wilson)**

Warren Price (Courtesy: Mary Walker Ward)

Glenn Walker
(All Photos Courtesy: Mary Walker Ward)

Sandy Dugger

Glenn Walker (Courtesy: Mary Walker Ward)

**Roan Valley, Butler, Glenn and Leona Walker home, Easter 1946:
Mary Walker and mother, Leona Dugger Walker
(Courtesy: Mary Walker Ward)**

, Butler, Main Street 1942: 1st row l-r Sara Whitehead, Mary Ann Ramsey, Anna Bess Trivette, Lorraine Millsaps, Wilma Dugger 2nd row l-r Edna Earle Honeycutt, Phyllis Greenwell, Helen DeBusk (Courtesy: Mary Walker Ward)

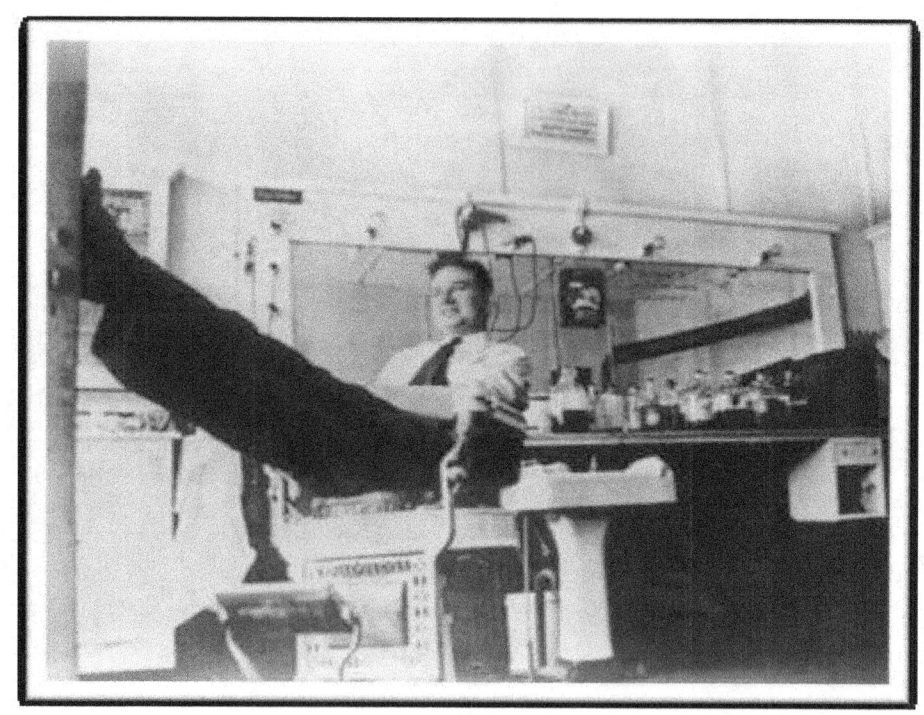

Butler 1940's: Kyle Stout (Courtesy: Joyce Dean Stout Garrison)

Watauga Valley, Spring Branch Hollow, Dry Hill: Fate Dugger
(Compiler Photo)

1905: Daniel Stout and Mary Holman Stout and grandson, Roby Stout (Courtesy: Nancy Fritts Tester)

Butler, 1930: Dr. David Swift (Courtesy: Florence Tucker)

Sugar Hollow 1953: Geraldine (Jean) Tester (Compiler Photos)

**Butler, 1930's: Monroe Phillips, (Old Roan Creek Bridge in background)
(All Photos Courtesy: Mary Walker Ward)**

Watauga River Bridge, Butler 1947: Edna Hyder, Ralph Hyder, Janet Greenwell

John Proffitt, Edna Hyder, Claude Potter, Ted Dugger, Jimmy Slemp
(All Photos Courtesy: Mary Walker Ward)

Janie Rainbolt Dugger

Watauga Lake, Roan Creek Dock 1950's: Jack Wilson, Sr. (Courtesy; Juanita Tester Wilson)

Roan Valley, 1930's: l-r Alice Wagner Jewett, R. G. Perkins Sr., Ester Wagner Perkins, Wallace Osborne
(Courtesy: R. G. Perkins Jr.)

Watauga Valley, Sugar Grove, 1920's: clockwise l-r Ella Anderson Cable, Levisey Cable Smith, William Cable, Raymond Cable, Thelma Irick, Arthur Irick (All Photos Courtesy: Juanita Tester Wilson)

Midway, 1951: l-r Herman Tester, Boyd Ward, Bob Ward, Steve Tester

Watauga Valley 1920's: l-r Stacy Main, Verdie Potter, Frank Lewis (All Photos Courtesy: Dee Tester)

Watauga River, Sugar Grove, 1942: Nell Baker and Ordie Cable Potter

WWII, 1943: William Andrew Duncan, Jr. (1922-2010)
(Courtesy: W.A. Duncan, Jr.)

Minerva Vaught (1813-1912) servant of Daniel B. Baker (1842-1932) and Sarah Vaught Baker (1846-1941); given to Mrs. Baker by her parents as a wedding present. All are interred in the Baker Gap Church Cemetery on property previously owned by the Bakers. (Courtesy: Juanita Tester Wilson)

Watauga Valley, Baker Gap 1920: Daniel Boone Baker with wife Sarah Vaught Baker and granddaughter Mary Louise Baker. (Courtesy: Juanita Tester Wilson)

Mr. Edward Grindstaff
(Courtesy: Juanita Tester Wilson)

Watauga Dam 1961: l-r Randal Laws, Michael Wilson, Robin Tester (Courtesy: Juanita Tester Wilson)

Opal Greenwell Boling (Courtesy: Dan Stansberry)

Butler 1940's: Raymond Pearson and Joe Dean (Courtesy: Florence Tucker)

Watauga Academy, James Hamilton Smith Monument, 1930's: Robert Devault Jr.
(Courtesy: Florence Tucker)

**Watauga Academy 1930's:
Mrs. Nat Hyder, Arvella Harmon and June Hyder
(Courtesy: Mary Walker Ward)**

**Midway 1950's: Bobby Wagner and Lewis Forrester
(Courtesy: Carolyn Tester Wagner)**

Butler, Watauga River Bridge with Roan Creek Bridge in background 1940's: Florence Tucker (Courtesy: Florence Tucker)

Watauga Valley, 1930's: Elbert Tucker (Courtesy: Florence Tucker)

**Watauga River Valley, Southern RR Bridge, 1940's: Florence Tucker and George Walker
(Courtesy: George Walker)**

Butler, Watauga Academy 1942: Mr. Clarence (Pete) Greever (Courtesy: Mary Walker Ward)

Midway, Dr. Elbert Forrester Home 1941: Carolyn Tester and Barton Forrester
(Courtesy: Carolyn Tester Wagner)

**Watauga Valley, Meal Camp Hollow 1930's: Carter Isaacs, Loy Isaacs, Nell Campbell
(Courtesy: Juanita Tester Wilson)**

**Watauga Lake, Roan Valley, Roan Creek Dock 1958: Jessie Wagner
(Courtesy: Carolyn Tester Wagner)**

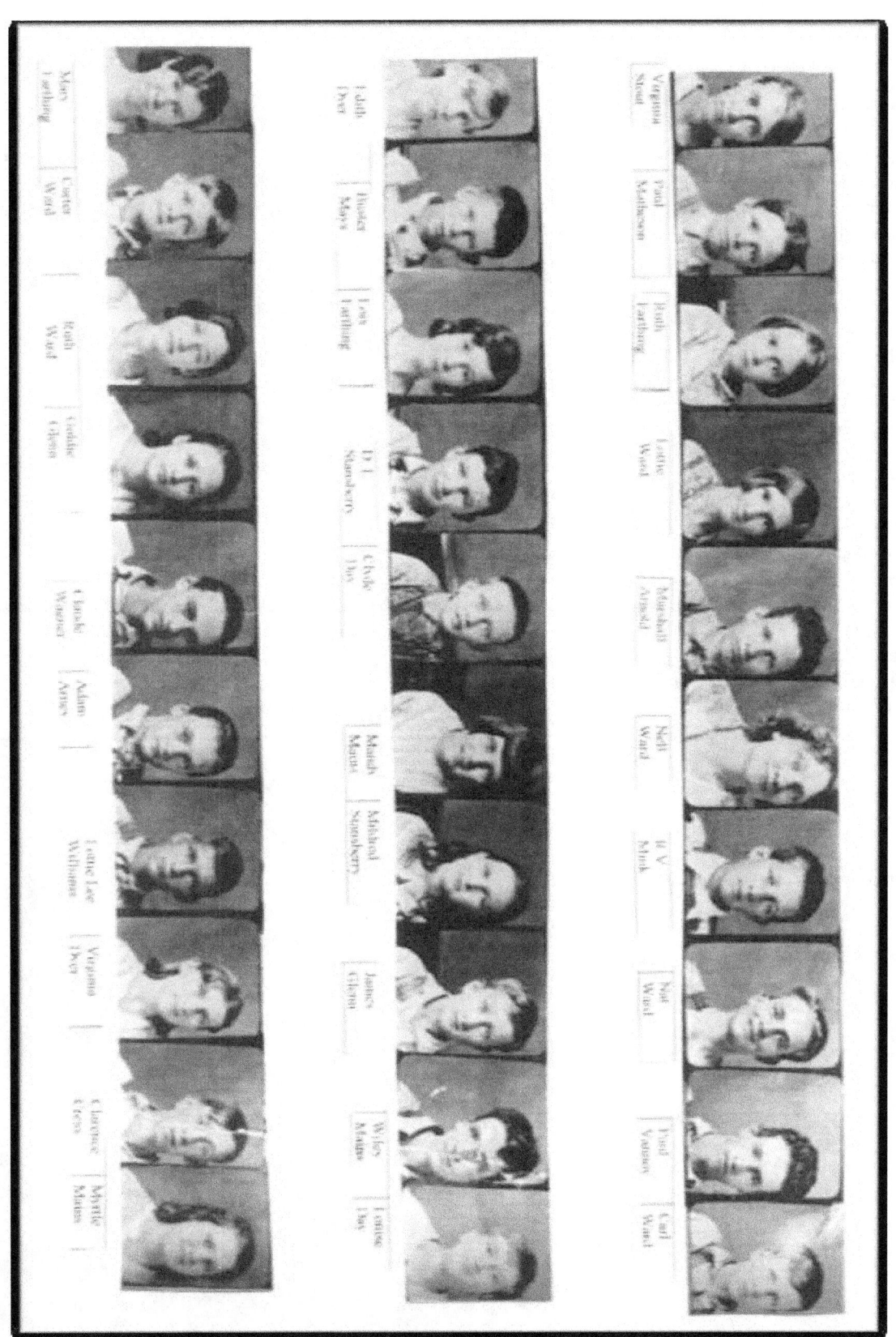

Roan Valley, Mill Creek, Pine Grove School 1930: students with teacher, Nell Ward
(Courtesy: Margaret Cress)

Watauga Valley: Home of John Isaac Reece (1853-1918) and Sarah Maples Reece (1859-1943) Interred in the Dugger Cemetery, Sugar Grove, Watauga Lake just up the valley from the location of their home. Fourteen children were born to the Isaac and Sarah including Brazilla Carroll Reece, long time congressman and soldier who served with distinction in World War I. Mrs. Reece's father, the Honorable L. L. Maples (1835-1917), founder of Enon Seminary, fore runner of the Watauga Academy is also interred in this cemetery. (All Photos Courtesy: Florence Tucker)

The Honorable Congressman, B. Carroll Reece

Roan Valley, Mill Creek: Mr. Clarence Cress   **Mr. Bob Cress**

Roan Valley, Mill Creek: Mr. Bob Cress (All Photos Courtesy: Margaret Cress)

Warren Tucker (Courtesy: Trula Pleasant Haley)

John Linville (Jack) Church (1859-1914) (Courtesy: Margaret Cress)

Rose Shull Hicks and Ann Cress (Courtesy: Margaret Cress)

R.H. Milhorn

(All Photos Courtesy: Anna Dugger Adkins)

Jim Milhorn

**Butler, early 1900's: Walter and Etta Crosswhite Griffey
(Courtesy: Bobby Wagner)**

Butler, 1943: Mrs. Blanch Gregg Ward and twins, Earl and Berl Ward (Courtesy: Bobby Jack Ward)

Ruth Griffey (Courtesy: Bobby Wagner)

Frank and Chloe Blackburn Jewett (Courtesy: Linda Tucker Jewett)

Carl Hollaway (Courtesy: Linda Tester Hollaway)

Roan Valley, Butler 1940's: Mrs. Leona Dugger Walker and Cindy (Courtesy: George Walker)

Butler, 1930: Florence Tucker and Ilean Dugger (Courtesy: Florence Tucker)

Paul Matheson (Compiler Photo)

Midway 1950's: Juanita Tester and Rosalie Bradley Mckinney: Stacy Grindstaff Home in right background, Beeler Stansberry's truck (Courtesy: Carolyn Tester Wagner)

Roan Valley, Maymead 1930: Robert Fritts and Brady Fritts (Courtesy: Nancy Fritts Tester)

Roan Valley, Neva 1910: Isaac Ward (1868-1933) and Molly Ward (1868-1954) and children including Clayt, Tip, Wheeler, Charlie, Minnie, Elmer and Azora. Mr. and Mrs. Ward are interred in the Brown Cemetery, Mill Creek at Pine Grove. (Courtesy: Bobby Jack Ward)

Elk Valley, 1920's: Park Main, Stacy Main and Loss Lewis (Courtesy: Linda Tester Hollaway)

Roan Valley 1940's: Elbert Wagner and Alice Grindstaff Wagner and children, Ray and Ester (Courtesy: Bobby Wagner)

**Preacher Samuel Carter DeLoach (1844-1920) and wife, Louise Garrison DeLoach (1844-1922). They are interred in the DeLoach Cemetery, Bee Hollow, Watauga Lake.
(Courtesy: Margaret Cress)**

Doe Mountain,, Hopper Branch 1930: Rosa, Bertie and Una Fritts (Courtesy: Una Fritts Glick)

Louise Greenwell Stansberry (All Photos Courtesy: Dan Stansberry)

Mr. Rod Greenwell

John Epperly, grandson of Esther Arney Epperly (Courtesy: Anna Dugger Adkins)

Choncy Campbell (Courtesy: Dan Stansberry)   **Haskell Tester (Courtesy: Larry Tester)**

Anna Lea Cable (Courtesy: Tammy Wilson Paul)

Anna Lea Cable Wilson and Tammy Wilson

Mamie and Lee Cable (All Photos Courtesy: Tammy Wilson Paul)

Watauga Valley, Little Milligan 1930's: Darlena McCloud Greenwell, Dale Greenwell, Bernice Greenwell
(Courtesy: Dan Stansberry)

**Dry Hill, Duncan Hollow 1951: Mr. Rod Greenwell and grandson, Dan Stansberry
(Courtesy: Dan Stansberry)**

Mildred Stansberry, Park Stout, Bernice Greenwell (Courtesy: Dan Stansberry)

**Dry Hill, Duncan Hollow 1930's: Greenwell sisters, Connie, Sylvia Horne and Jane
(All Photos Courtesy: Dan Stansberry)**

**Bernice Greenwell Stout
and Park Stout**

Roan Valley, Little Dry Run 1950's: Emma Lou Bradley (Courtesy: Dan Stansberry)

Watauga Valley, Cowanstown 1952: l-r Frankie Church, Iris Greer, Grace Dean, Francis Cannon (Compiler Photo)

United States Army Signal Corps 1954: Herman Tester (Compiler Photo)

**Watauga Valley, Cowantown,: children of Frank and Pearl Burton Bunton
l-r Ruth, Raymond, Dwight, Asa, Martha, Scott)**

**Watauga Valley 1925:
Dove Burton
(All Photos Courtesy: Martha Bunton Query)**

Roan Valley, Mill Creek 1945: Edwin Matheson (Courtesy: Claude Matheson)

Raymond Coppenger
(Courtesy: Raymond Coppenger)

Butler Baptist Church 1950: l-r M.H. Carder, James Gregg, B. Carroll Reece, Brown Bowers, Raymond Coppenger, G. H. Glass, Ralph Hyder, Coy Riddle, Hilton Powell, Ben Wood (Compiler Photo)

Roan Valley, Neva, Fritts Store 1950's: Mr. Bob Fritts (Courtesy: Nancy Fritts Tester)

Roan Valley, Neva 1930's: Brady Fritts (Courtesy: Una Fritts Glick)

Glen Smith Greenwell and Roderick Greenwell (All Photos Courtesy: Dan Stansberry)

WW II: D.L. Stansberry, Sr.

Doe Mountain, Hopper Branch 1932: Una and Rosa Fritts (Courtesy: Una Fritts Glick)

Louise Greenwell (Courtesy: Dan Stansberry)

Nelson Tester (Courtesy: Juanita Tester Wilson)

l-r Emma Lou Bradley, Buster Jewett, Carolyn Tester, Eleanor Kimberlin, Lewis Forrester, Mary Lea Fletcher (Courtesy: Carolyn Tester Wagner)

Roan Valley, Neva 1930's: Hal Shull and family (Courtesy: Louise McQueen Shull)

Cobb Creek 1920': Robert (Bob) Matheson (Courtesy: Barbara Henley Styles)

Neva, Maymead, Pleasant Grove Baptist Church 1950's: l-r back Opal Tester, Hallie Madron, Hazel Hodge, Karen Grindstaff, Barbara Maze, Ethel Hodge, l-r front Steve Snyder, Ann Brown, Teresa Simcox, Betty Sue Warren, Billy Worley (Courtesy: Alma Ward Worley)

Watauga Academy Teacher and Advisor, Miss Margaret Dougherty

(Courtesy: Anna Dugger Adkins)

Roan Valley, Neva, Maymead 1950: George Washington Fritts and Nettie Lunceford Fritts
(Courtesy: Louise McQueen Shull)

**Doe Mountain, Hopper Branch 1940's:
Nettie Lunceford Fritts**
(Courtesy: Nancy Fritts Tester)

Midway Service Station 1950:
Issac Cable (1901-1975).
Son of John and Jane Greenwell Cable, interred in the Cable Cemetery, Sugar Grove, Watauga with his wife, Hessie White Cable (1905-1980).
(Compiler Photo)

Watauga Valley, Cowantown 1956: Children of Frank and Pearl Burton Bunton l-r Ruth, Raymond, Martha, Scott, Dwight, Asa (Courtesy: Martha Bunton Query)

Butler City School, 1927 Primer, 1st and 2nd graders:
1st row l-r Hazel McElyea, Fred Mary, Jack McQueen, Robert Nave, Helen Ward, Edwina McQueen, Laverne Sheffield, Marjorie Moore, Helen Neatherly, Verna Lee Wolfe, Dovie Eggers, Helen Sheffield. 2nd row l-r J. C. Norris, Lacy Stout, Edwin DeVault, Louise Tucker, Vernell Courtner, Doris Atwood, Lois Burton, Fay Norris, Billy Joe Lineback, Anne Von Cannon, 3rd row l-r Lacy Pilk, Earl Presnell, Fleenor Stout, Ellis Tucker, Louise Birchfield, Elana Campbell, Lida Cable, Vivian Reed, and Christine Whitehead. Peggy O'Neil, teacher (Courtesy: Louise Tucker Pleasant)

Elk Valley, Lower Elk 1945: Hattie Cook Hicks and Lawrence Hicks (Compiler Photo)

**Midway, 1952: Bobby Wagner
(Courtesy: Carolyn Tester Wagner)**

Watauga Valley, 1939: Scott Bunton, Martha Bunton, Asa Bunton, Dwight Bunton, Raymond Bunton and Ruth Bunton (Courtesy: Martha Bunton Query)

Dry Hill, Duncan Hollow 1960's: Rod and Glenn Greenwell (Courtesy: Dan Stansberry)

Watauga Valley, Cowantown 1900: Millard Scott Burton (Courtesy: Martha Bunton Query)

1913: l-r Ruth Burton, Pearl Burton, Martha Burton and Paul Burton (Courtesy: Martha Bunton Query)

Stout Branch 1920's: D. L. Stansberry (Courtesy: Dan Stansberry)

Watauga Valley, Sugar Grove 1943: John Cable (Courtesy: Martha Bunton Query)

Stephen Justice Brown Family 1895: Seated Stephen and Addie Wagner Brown and children l-r Thomas, Charlie, Addie Lee and Talulah (Courtesy: Louise McQueen Shull)

Alonzo Pearson Glenn (1878-1922). Interred in Brown Cemetery, Mill Creek at Pine Grove with his wife Myrtle G. Glenn (1885-1961). (Courtesy: Shirley Glenn Stout)

Roan Valley Robert and Hattie Milhorn Home 1940's:
Harold, Billy and Tommy Milhorn
and mother, Hattie in back (Courtesy: Anna Dugger Adkins)

Douglas Bradley, son
of Norvan (Nub) Bradley and Lena
Mae Kimberlin Bradley
(Compiler Photo)

Roan Valley, Neva 1920's: Sallie Alice Matheson (Courtesy: Nancy Fritts Tester)

Dick Pleasant (Compiler Photos)

Trula Pleasant

Roan Valley, Fritts Curve 1939: Pauline Laws and Elsie Fritts (Compiler Photo)

Elk Valley, Elk Mills 1940's: Gladys Pearson (Courtesy: Mary Walker Ward)

**Rachel Bailey Matheson, 1ⁿᵈ wife of Henry Harold Matheson;
older sister of Mr. Matheson's 2ˢᵗ wife, Nancy Bailey Matheson
(Courtesy: Nancy Fritts Tester)**

Will M. Slimp and Nancy Bailey (Courtesy: Nancy Fritts Tester)

Stout Branch 1946:
Earl, Edwin and Beatrice
Simcox Matheson
(Courtesy: Claude Matheson)

Roan Valley, Neva, 1950's: Earl Shull (All Photos Courtesy: Nancy Fritts Tester)

Roan Valley, Neva 1950's: sisters, Barbara Shull and Patsy Shull

**Paris, France 1945: Brothers, Barton Matheson and Claude Matheson
(Courtesy: Nancy Fritts Tester)**

Butler, Watauga Academy 1930's: Norman Dugger (Courtesy: Florence Tucker)

Wylie Neil Stout and Sallie Stout Walker (Courtesy: Nancy Fritts Tester)

Fina Greenwell Duncan (Courtesy: Dan Stansberry)

**Watauga Valley, Sugar Grove 1920's: Twin Twins, Doris and Dorothy DeVault, Alta and Alma Cable
(Courtesy: Dee Cable Tester)**

Norman Dugger (Compiler Photo)

Butler Bridge, 1946:

Edna Hyder, Mary Walker (Courtesy: Mary Walker Ward)

Butler, 1946: Jimmy Griffitts
(Courtesy: Mary Walker Ward)

Little Dry Run, Midway 1950's: K.E. (Goose) Bradley, Zola Kimberlin Bradley, Jack Cable, Rosemary Bradley and Charles Bradley (Courtesy: Jack Cable)

Midway, W. T. Bradley Farm 1950's: Roscoe Forrester, Reverend Minton, Zola Kimberlin Bradley, K.E. (Goose) Bradley, Clifford Kimberlin and W. T. Bradley (Courtesy: Jack Cable)

Jack Cable   (Compiler Photos)   **Charles Bradley**

Johnson County Bus Drivers 1960 (Compiler Photos)

1960 Luke Tester

Mr. Charles Monroe McCloud and dog, Mike. (Courtesy: Thomas C. McCloud)

Maymead, Neva 1954: Patsy Shull and Nancy Fritts (Courtesy: Nancy Fritts Tester)

Midway 1952: Beeler Stansberry (Courtesy: Carolyn Tester Wagner)

Roan Valley, Neva 1940's, Bob Fritts Store: Children of Earl and Louise McQueen Shull l-r Tom, Patsy, Linda, Barbara (Courtesy: Louise McQueen Shull)

Neva 1900: George and Sallie Bradley Ward and children, Paul and Earl (Courtesy: Alma Ward Worley)

Watauga River Valley 1930's: Wayne Smith (Compiler Photo)

Midway Boat Dock 1962: Robin Eric Tester (Compiler Photo)

Betty and Barton Matheson (Courtesy: Claude Matheson)

Stout Branch 1920's: D. L., Mildred and Vada Stansberry (Courtesy: Dan Stansberry)

Watauga Valley 1930's: Lucille Conway, Loyd Gregg, Carter Isaacs, Linell Gregg
(Courtesy: Juanita Tester Wilson)

Roan Valley, Stout Branch 1940's: Catherine Stout Matheson
(Courtesy: Claude Matheson)

Midway 1950's: Ad and Eddy Kimberlin (Courtesy: Eleanor Kimberlin Church)

Roan Valley, Fritts Curve 1940's: Martha Snyder Fritts and Charles Fritts
(Courtesy: Nancy Fritts Tester)

Watauga Valley, Cowantown 1920's:
Haskel Isaacs, Faye Triplette Isaacs, Wallace Dugger, Elsie Gregg Dugger
(Courtesy: Juanita Tester Wilson)

Betty Ann Dugger Cable (1889-1972) and Isaac Columbus Cable (1877-1963), (Courtesy Shirley Hooper)

Martha May Ellis and Daniel Ellis (Courtesy: Juanita Tester Wilson)

Watauga River, Sugar Grove 1943: Isaac Cable, Juanita Tester, Olis (Joe Bill) Cable, Ordie Potter, Herman Tester, Lucille Conway, Dexter Forrester, Charlene Tester, Lorene Forrester, Nell Baker Carolyn Tester, Luke Tester, Dee Tester, Anna Ruth Cable (Courtesy: Juanita Tester Wilson)

**Watauga Valley, Sugar Grove 1940: Lucille Conway, Carolyn Tester, Charlene Tester, George Potter
(All Photos Courtesy: Juanita Tester Wilson)**

Nancy Rebecca Greenwell Dugger

**Glenn and Leona Walker farm 1942,: Lawrence Dugger and mother, Ida Rainbolt Dugger
(Courtesy: Mary Walker Ward)**

Callie Slimp Snyder (1870-1955)
Interred Slimp Cemetery Roan Creek Butler
(Courtesy: Nancy Fritts Tester)

Elk Valley, Sugar Hollow 1935: Victor Trivette, Ruby Tester, Ruth Tester, Howard Tester
(Courtesy: Ruth Tester Jones)

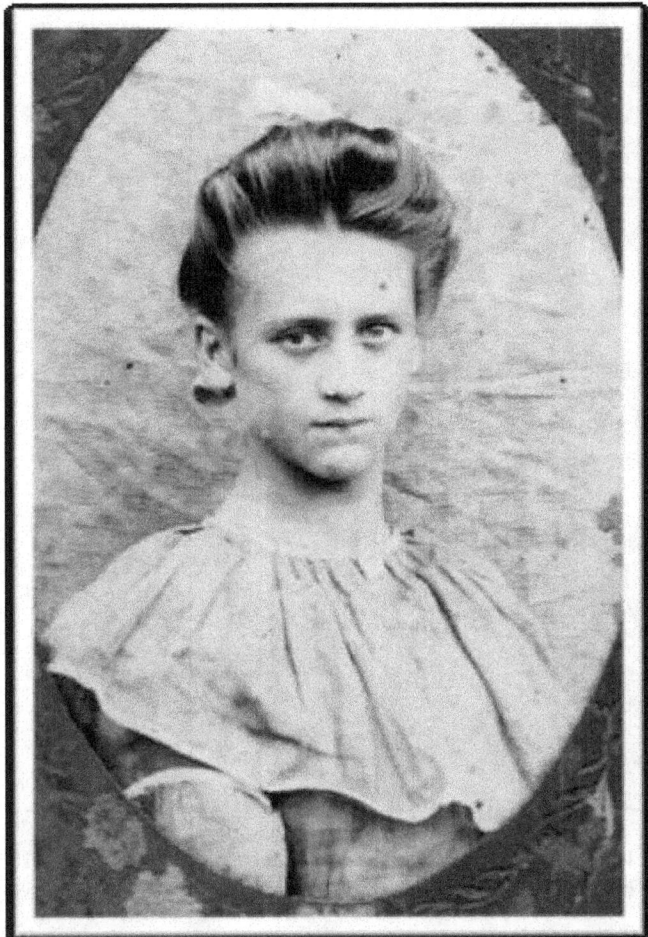

Effie Ellen Snyder Robinson 1903-1931)
Interred in the Joe Robinson Cemetery,
Pine Orchard, Butler with husband
James Kyle Robinson (1903-1953)
(Courtesy: Nancy Fritts Tester)

Floyd A. Snyder Jr. (1931-1951)
Interred in the Snyder Cemetery, Roan Creek
(Compiler Photo)

William and Amanda Cable Greenwell and children, l-r Ira, Asa, William, Godfrey, Amanda, Glen and Effie
(Courtesy: Shirley Hooper)

John D. Snyder
(Courtesy:
Nancy Fritts Tester)

Lafayette Snyder
(Courtesy: Nancy Fritts Tester)

Bert Isaacs and Martha Anderson Isaacs
(Courtesy: Juanita Tester Wilson)

Thomas Houston and Nancy Jane Cable and children
l-r Alvin, Isaac, Thomas Houston, Ellen, Nancy Jane, Sarah, Mary, Alice
(Courtesy: Shirley Hooper)

1st row l-r, Tom Baker, Lou Bunton Baker, James Cable, Mary Smith Cable, Tom Cable
2nd row l-r, Nancy Cable, Thean Cable, Sarah Cable, Oam Cable, Tiltie Cable, David Cable
(Courtesy: Juanita Tester Wilson)

Loranza Boone Cable (1905-1988)
(Courtesy: Shirley Hooper)

Laurel Fork, Rominger, NC 1917: Home of Eli Finley Tester and Camoline Presnell Tester. In photo 1st row l-r: Luke Tester, Earl Tester, Rilda Tester Campbell, Charlie Mast, Daisy Presnell, Finley Pearce Tester, Ida Tester Finney, Eli Finley Tester 2nd row l-r: Rebecca Yates, Hessie Hicks Presnell, Luna Presnell Baird, Aner Tester Rominger, Coy Rominger, Alpha Hicks Presnell, Birdie Mast Ward, Coy Tester, Eller Presnell Love, Henry Haganan 3rd row l-r: Maud Mast Harmon, Boyd Harmon, Conley Harmon, Smith Tester. Also located here was a store and post office owned by the Testers. Camoline served as postmaster for Laurel Fork. The home burned in 1919 and the Testers moved to Carter and Johnson Counties in Tennessee. Camoline (1880-1947) and E.F. (1872-1954) are interred in the Andrews-Tester Cemetery in the Sugar Hollow on the property they previously owned. (Courtesy: Juanita Tester Wilson)

Elk Valley, Elk Mills 1924: Alice Green Walsh, Roddy Walsh and Gladys Walsh
(Courtesy: Juanita Tester Wilson)

Watauga Valley, Sugar Grove 1905: sisters Vernie Mae Anderson, Cora Anderson and Louie Anderson, daughters of Ezra Oliver Anderson (1855-1926) and Nancy Clawson Anderson (1854-1925). The Andersons are interred in the Sugar Grove Church Cemetery, Watauga Lake, Butler (Courtesy: Juanita Tester Wilson)

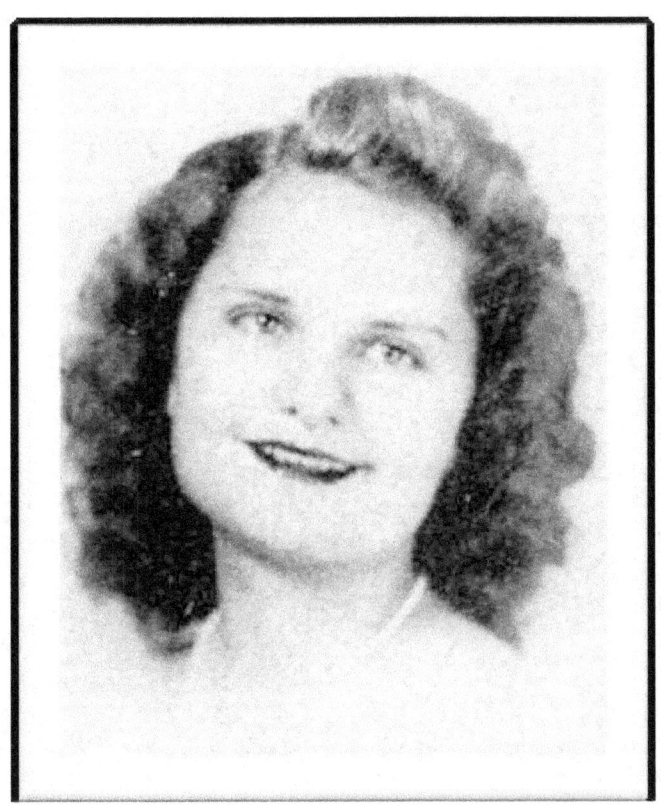

Watauga Academy 1948: Edna Earle Honeycutt (Compiler Photos)

Watauga Academy 1948: Paul Courtner

Celia Simerly McKinney and William McKinney (Courtesy: Juanita Tester Wilsonr)

Watauga Academy 1948:
Bill Wolfe
(Compiler Photo)

**Laurel Fork NC 1917:
Earl Tester and Luna Presnell Baird
(Courtesy: Juanita Tester Wilson)**

Sugar Hollow 1920's: adults l-r: Susan Presnell Presnell, Aner Tester Rominger, Camoline Presnell Tester (1880-1947), Eli Finley Tester (1872-1954) children l-r:Bobby Rominger, Howard Tester, Mae Tester, Ruth Tester. Mr. and Mrs. Tester are interred in the Andrews-Tester Cemetery in the Sugar Hollow on property they once owned. (Courtesy: Juanita Tester Wilson)

Roan Valley, Stout Branch 1940's: John Henry Matheson (Courtesy: Claude Matheson)

Wiley Smith
(Courtesy: Juanita Tester Wilson)

Watauga Academy 1948:
Jack Dugger
(Compiler Photo)

The Tucker Boys 1930's: front Warren and Ellis, back Elbert, Troy and Charles
(Courtesy: Louise Tucker Pleasant)

Midway Baptist Sunday School Class, 1952: Mrs. Texe Forrester, teacher. From left
Lewis Forrester, Emma Lou Bradley, Jim Kimberlin, Carolyn Tester, Ed Grindstaff,
Juanita Tester, Herman Tester, Eleanor Kimberlin, Mrs. Forrester.
(Courtesy: Juanita Tester Wilson)

Watauga Academy 1939: J. C. Smith (Compiler Photo)

**Loyd F. Heaton (1924-1978) U. S. Army World War II.
Interred in the Bakers Gap Cemetery, Big Dry Run, Butler
(Courtesy: Naomi Heaton and William Arnold)**

Roan Valley, Fritts Curve 1905: Martha Slemp and her father, William Wiley Slemp
(Courtesy: Nancy Fritts Tester)

Roan Valley, Fritts Curve 1960's: Nell Fritts (Courtesy: Nancy Fritts Tester)

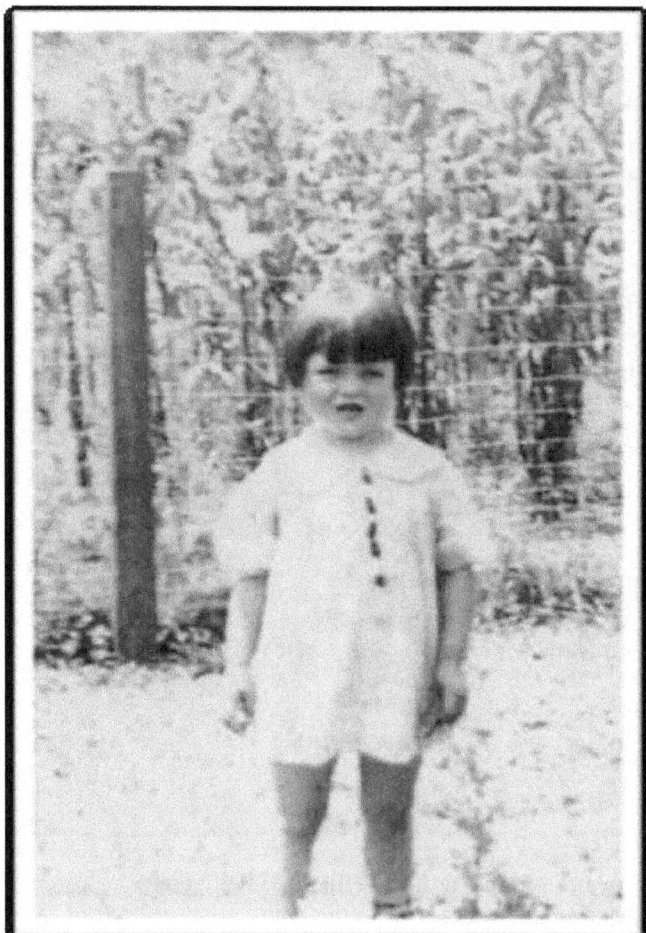

Elk River Valley 1938: Mary Jo Main
(All Photos Courtesy: Juanita Tester Wilson)

Ordie Cable Potter, Alta Cable Triplett

Watauga Valley, Sugar Grove 1940's: Josie Laws Cable and sons, Frank, Larry and Richard (Courtesy: Juanita Tester Wilson)

Shouns School, Early Spring 1950: , Bus to Lower End from Johnson County High School
l-r Edward Gridnstaff, Herman Tester, Jack Cable, Vestal Cowan (Compiler Photo)

Watauga Academy 1945: Teachers Alma Worley and Betty Early (Courtesy; Florence Tucker)

Hopper Branch 1920's: Robert Brownlow (Bob) Fritts (Courtesy: Nancy Fritts Tester)

Bruce Stevens (Courtesy: Nancy Fritts Tester)

1930's Watauga Valley: Asa, Martha and Scott Bunton

**Millard Scott Burton and Rebecca Bunton Burton family 1917:
l-r Dove, Pearl, Scott, Paul, Rose, Rebecca, Ruth, Martha
(All Photos Courtesy: Martha Bunton Query)**

Isaac Columbus Cable and Betty Ann Dugger Cable and family back l-r Beulah (1918-2005) David (1925-2007) Boone (1916-1992) Freda (1914-1996) Glenn (1923-2000) Janie (1910-2001) Tom (1920-1957) front l-r Mollie (1927-) Isaac Columbus (1877-1963) Martha Jean (1930-) Betty Ann (1889-1972)
(Courtesy: Shirley Hooper)

Millard Scott Burton and Rebecca Bunton Burton family 1930:
l-r Scott, Paul, Rebecca, Ruth, Pearl, Dove, Martha, Rose (Courtesy: Martha Bunton Query)

Roan Valley, Rock Springs 1951:
Nell Fritts
(Courtesy: Nancy Fritts Tester)

**Roan Valley, Stout Branch 1919: Harrison Stansberry, Jessie Stout Stansberry with son D. L.
(Courtesy: Dan Stansberry)**

Parker Main, Jr. and sister Mary Jo Main (Courtesy: Juanita Tester Wilson)

Roan Valley, Rock Springs 1950's: l-r Martha Snyder Fritts, Charlie Fritts, Violet Fritts, Wiley Fritts, Elsie Fritts, Nell Fritts
(Courtesy: Nancy Fritts Tester)

Claude Millsaps (Compiler Photos)

**Watauga Valley, Big Dry Run, Dry Run School 1950's: Randy Gene and Archie Dean Stout
(Courtesy: Dan Stansberry)**

Butler, Glenn and Leona Walker Home 1946: Gladys Pearson (Courtesy: Mary Walker Ward)

James H. Jenkins (Courtesy: Mary Walker Ward)

Watauga Valley, Fish Springs/Piercetown Bridge 1930's: Park Stout and Bernice Greenwell
(Courtesy Dan Stansberry)

Roan Valley 1930: sisters, Jessie Stout Stansberry and Emily (Emma) Stout Grindstaff and Elsie Stansberry
(Courtesy: Dan Stansberry)

**Roan Valley, Stout Branch 1940's:
Louise Hackney
(Courtesy: Claude Matheson)**

**1863 Union Army: William Harrison Bunton
(Courtesy: Martha Bunton Query)**

Thomas Watson and Hattie Watson, sister and brother (Courtesy: Juanita Tester Wilson)

Loutisha Clark Greenwell and
Henry Thomas Greenwell
(Courtesy: Dan Stansberry)

**Roan Creek Restaurant, Watauga Lake 1950's: Juanita Tester and Jack Wilson, Jr.
(Courtesy: Juanita Tester Wilson)**

Roan Valley, Maymead 1920's: Sarafina Wagner McQueen (1858-1930) widow of Isaac W. McQueen (1805-1890) with three of her five children. l-r Thomas McQueen born 1888, Sarafina, Rebecca McQueen Shull born 1879 and Joseph McQueen born 1886. Her other children were Mary born 1884 and Isaac born 1886. Mrs. Sarafina McQueen was a mother at 21 and a widow at 31 with five young children. She continued to manage the large farm until her death of pneumonia at the age of 72 in 1930. Her grandchildren and great grandchildren continue to own and live on the original farm which remains productive.
(Courtesy: Louise McQueen Shull)

Roan Valley, Dry Hill 1940's: Brothers, D.L. Stansberry, Elcaney Isaacs, David Ray Stansberry
(All Photos Courtesy: Dan Stansberry)

Roan Valley, Stout Branch 1930's: Harrison Stansberry and Jessie Stout Stansberry Family
back row l-r David Ray, Mildred, D.L., Vada, front row l-r Harrison holding James, Jessie and Lucille

**Thomas Jefferson Cable (1871-1953) and Jane Cannon Cable (1872-1941)
Interred Cable Cemetery at Dorton in Pike County, Kentucky (Courtesy: Juanita Tester Wilson)**

Hazel Ward Shull (Compiler Photo)

Watauga Academy 1948: Carter Isaacs

(Compiler Photos)

Watauga Academy 1948: Denver Forrester

Watauga Valley, Sugar Grove 1930's: Delia Cable Cable (1882-1968) and father, John Cable (1858-1952) Both interred in Cable Cemetery, Sugar Grove, Watauga Lake.(Courtesy: Juanita Tester Wilson)

John Baker Cable Jr. "Little John" (1855-1939) Interred Cable Cemetery, Swain County NC
(Courtesy: Juanita Tester Wilson)

Elk Valley, Stout Hill 1930's: Shafter Stout (1916-1994) Interred in the John Stout Family Cemetery, Elk Mills and Milda Isaacs Stout (1918-   ) (Courtesy: Juanita Tester Wilson)

Watauga Valley, Sugar Grove 1948: l-r Alta Cable Triplett with daughter Linda Triplett, Nettie Cable Main with granddaughter Penny Sue Tester, Douglas Laws with grandmother Dee Cable Tester, Patty Potter with grandmother Ordie Cable Potter (Courtesy: Juanita Tester Wilson)

Watauga Academy 1948: Selma 'Babe' Curtis, Music Teacher (Compiler Photo)

Watauga Valley, Sugar Grove 1905: William Cable (1869-1930)and Ella Anderson Cable (1876-1940) and children, Ordie (born 1904) Dewey(born 1899) Nettie (born 1897)and Annie (born 1902) (Courtesy: Juanita Tester Wilson)

Winnie Walker Goodwin and Lee Goodwin (Courtesy: Mary Walker Ward)

Watauga Valley, Sugar Grove, 1920's Whiting Railroad Water Tank: Austin Hollaway, Glen Dugger home in background (Courtesy: Linda Tester Hollaway)

Midway 1950's: Jean Tester, Carolyn Tester, Juanita Tester, Eleanor Kimberlin (Courtesy: Carolyn Tester Wagner)

Watauga Valley, Sugar Grove, Whiting Railroad Water Tank 1920's: l-r Austin Hollaway, McKinley Laws, Mack Tester, Glenn Dugger (Courtesy: Linda Tester Hollaway)

Abner and Mary Lunceford Lowe (Courtesy: Alma Ward Worley)

**Dry Hill, Duncan Hollow 1960's: front Lennis Greer, Steven Tester back Dee Cable Tester, Luke Tester
(Courtesy: Carolyn Tester Wagner)**

**Watauga Valley, 1910's: Ben H. Isaacs (1888-1974)
Interred in Sugar Grove Church Cemetery, Watauga Lake**

John Main (All Photos Courtesy: Juanita Tester Wilson)

Butler, 1940's Birthday Party Group for David Stout (Courtesy: Mary Walker Ward)

Bernice Greenwll and Parker Stout (Courtesy: Dan Stansberry)

Watauga Valley 1940's: Flora Gregg Isaacs married Ben H. Isaacs 1915.
Interred Sugar Grove Baptist Church Cemetery, Watauga Lake
(Courtesy: Juanita Tester Wilson)

**Lucinda Isaacs (1891-1974) and Lafayette Burton (1892-1984) married 1916.
Interred in the HappyValley Memorial Park, Elizabethton
(Courtesy: Juanita Tester Wilson)**

Watauga Valley, Fish Springs 1922: Retha Smith (1903-1926). Wife of Joe H. Smith interred in the Union Baptist Church Cemetery, Dividing Ridge, Hampton (Courtesy: Mary Jo Main)

**Midway 1955: l-r Steven Tester, Bobby Wagner, Billy Joe Wagner; in auto Pat Tester and Connie Wagner
(Courtesy: Carolyn Tester Wagner)**

Midway 1952: Luke Tester and Lewis Forrester (Courtesy: Carolyn Tester Wagner)

Watauga Valley, Sugar Grove 1900: back l-r William Christopher Columbus Greenwell (1873-1932) Amanda Cable Greenwell (1872-1952) Asa (1900-1991) front William Terrell Greenwell (187-1911) Ira (1897-1980) Elizabeth Dugger Greenwell (1837-1907) Benjamin D.Cable (1835-1918) Effie (1898-1991) Susannah Simerly Cable (1836-1920) (Courtesy: Juanita Tester Wilson)

Howard Smith and mother, Vicey Cable Smith seated;
standing Beulah Smith Caldwell, Fannie Smith and Pearl Smith daughters of Vicey Smith
(Courtesy: Juanita Tester Wilson)

William Arnold (Courtesy: Naomi Heaton and William Arnold)

1930's Advertisement for City of Butler (Compiler Photo)

MAPS FOR USE WITH
(Courtesy: George Walker)

PORTRAIT OF THE PAST

1920's Advertisement for D.A. Davis Store at Vaughtsville (Courtesy: Alma Ward Worley)

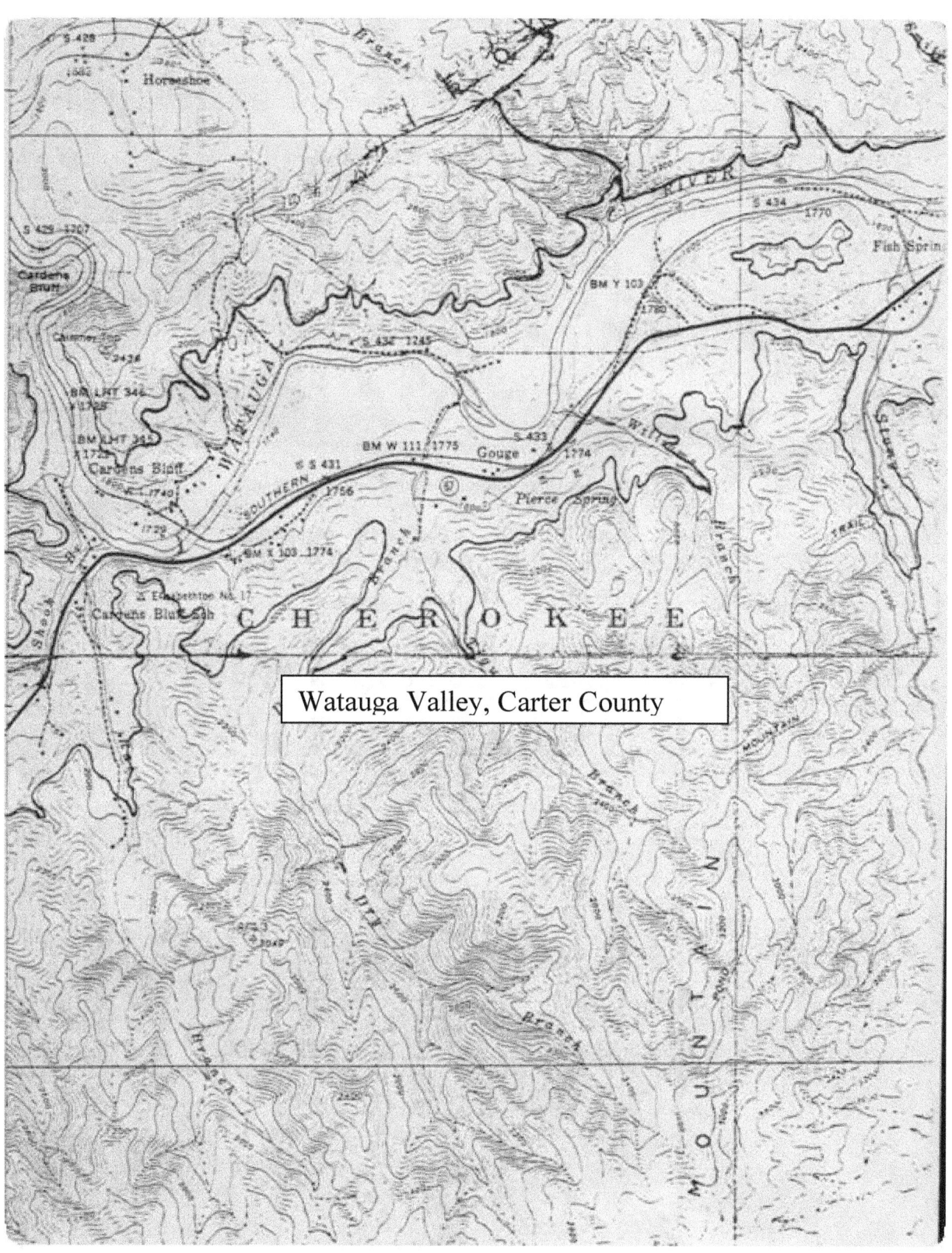

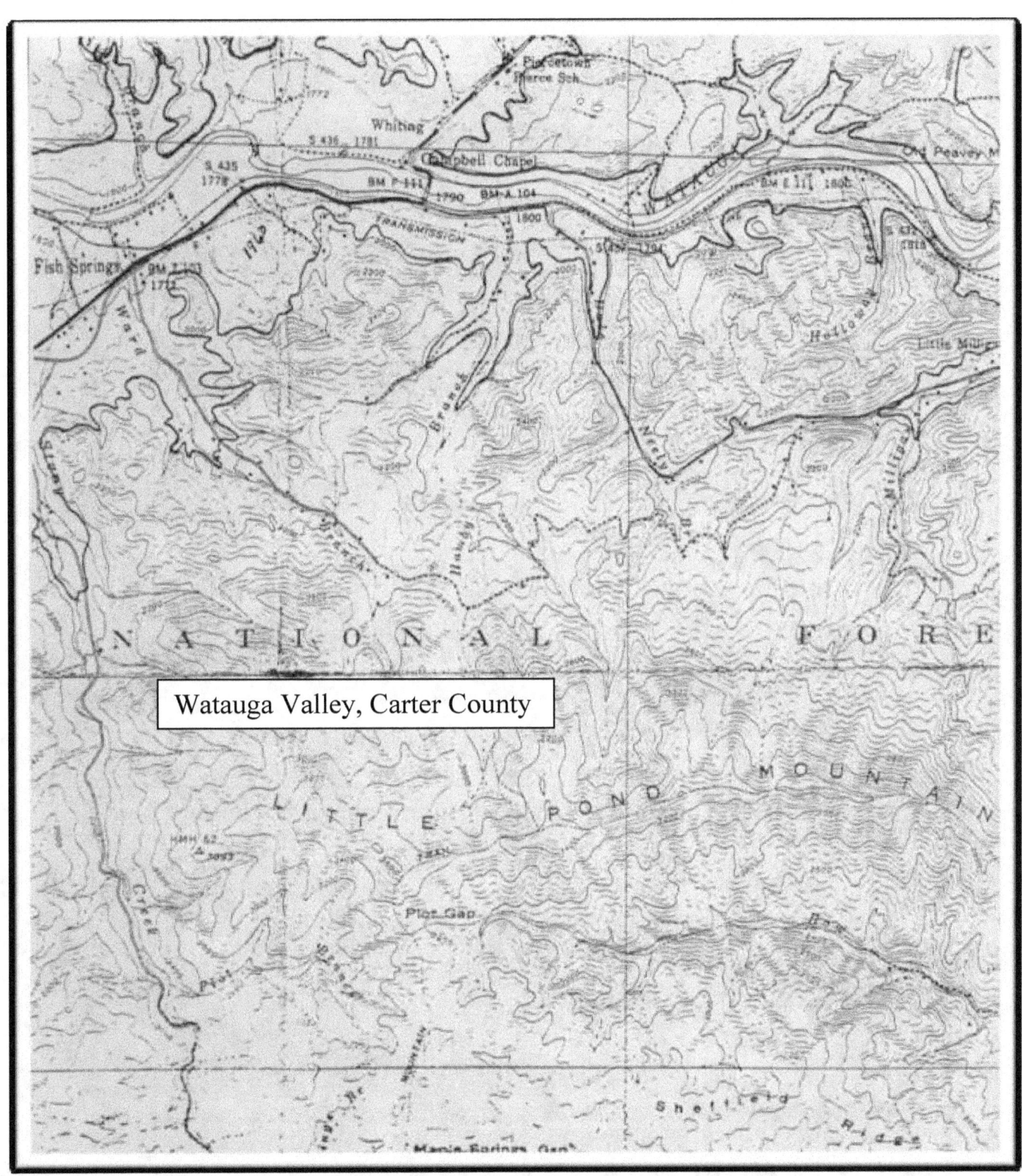
Watauga Valley, Carter County

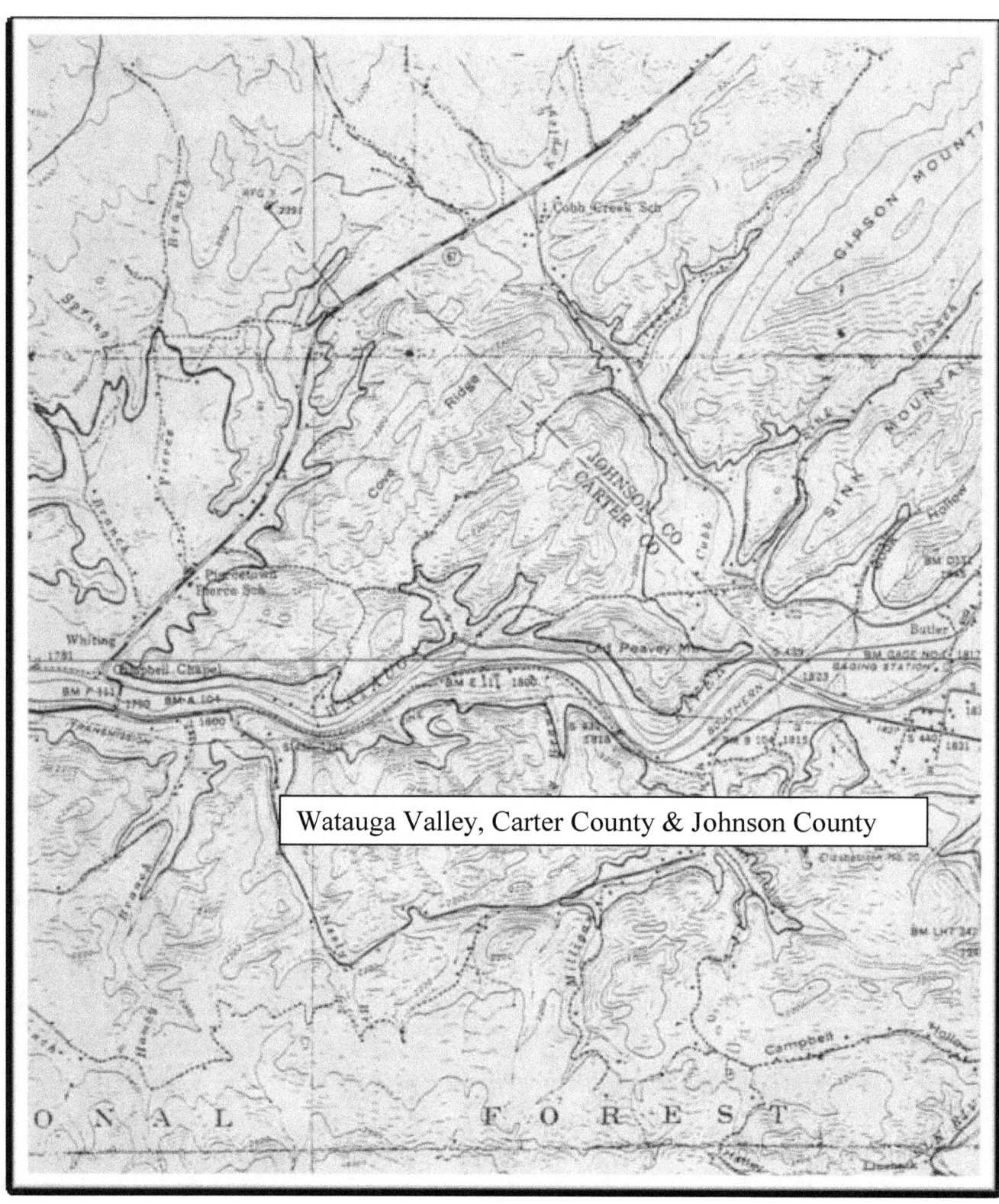
Watauga Valley, Carter County & Johnson County

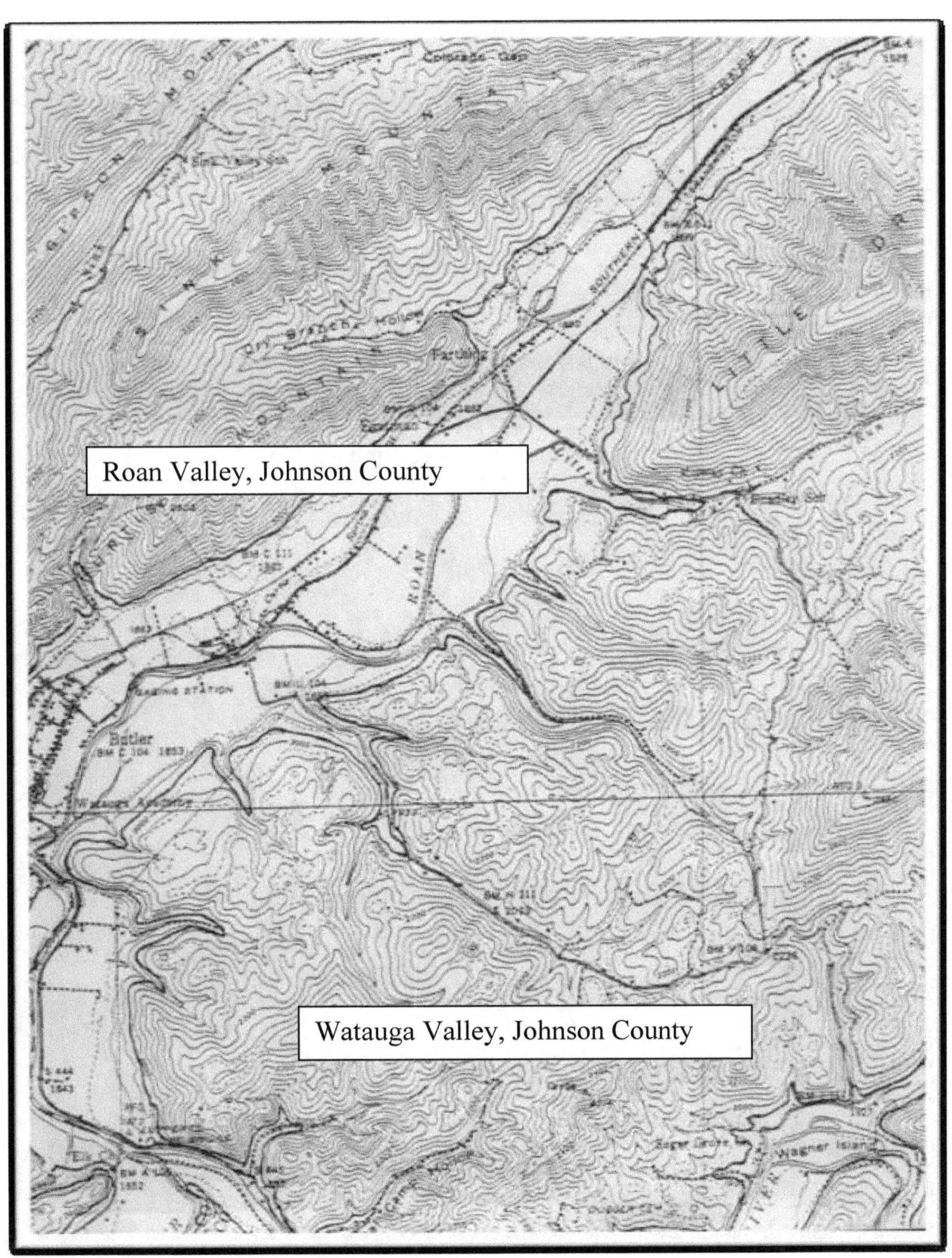

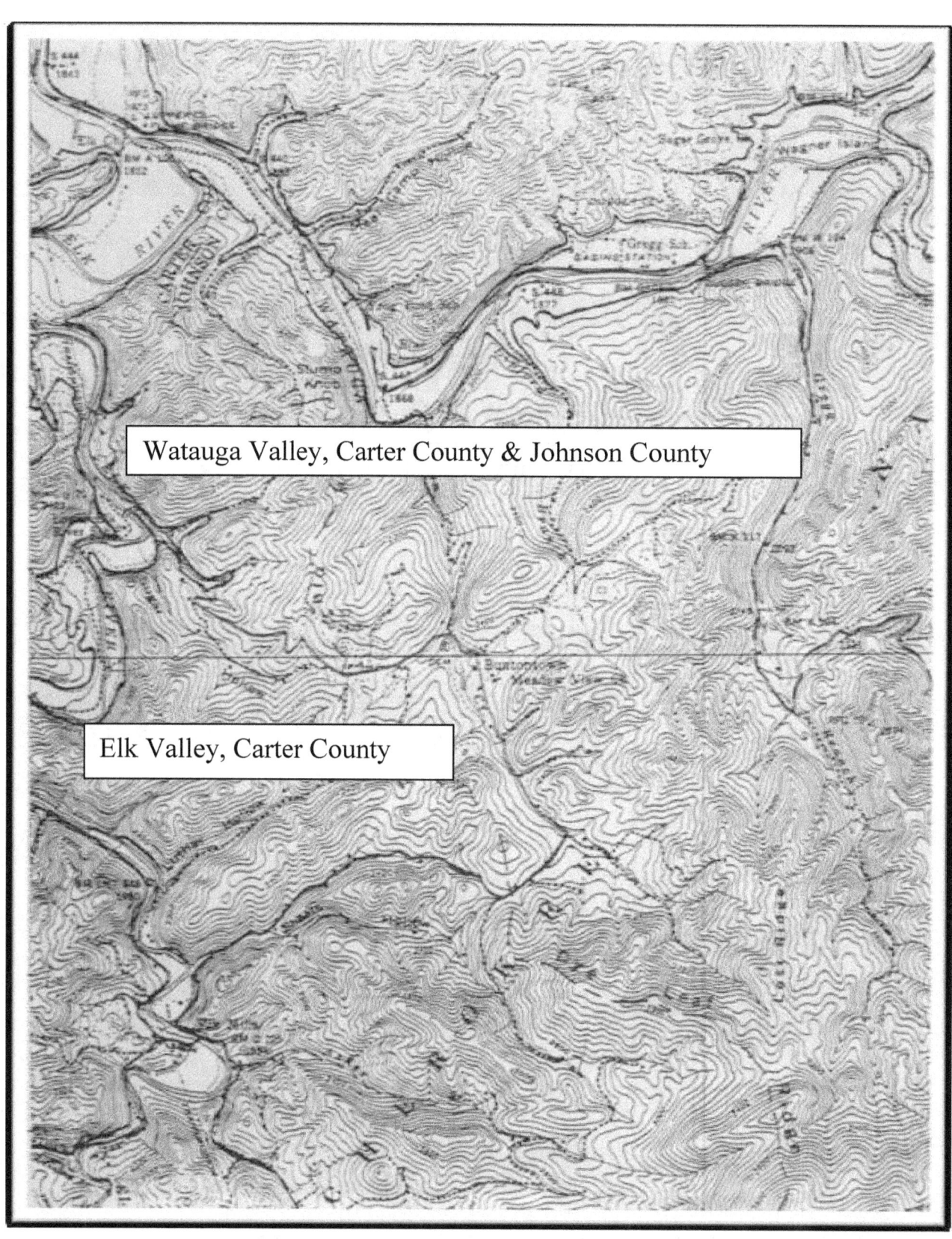

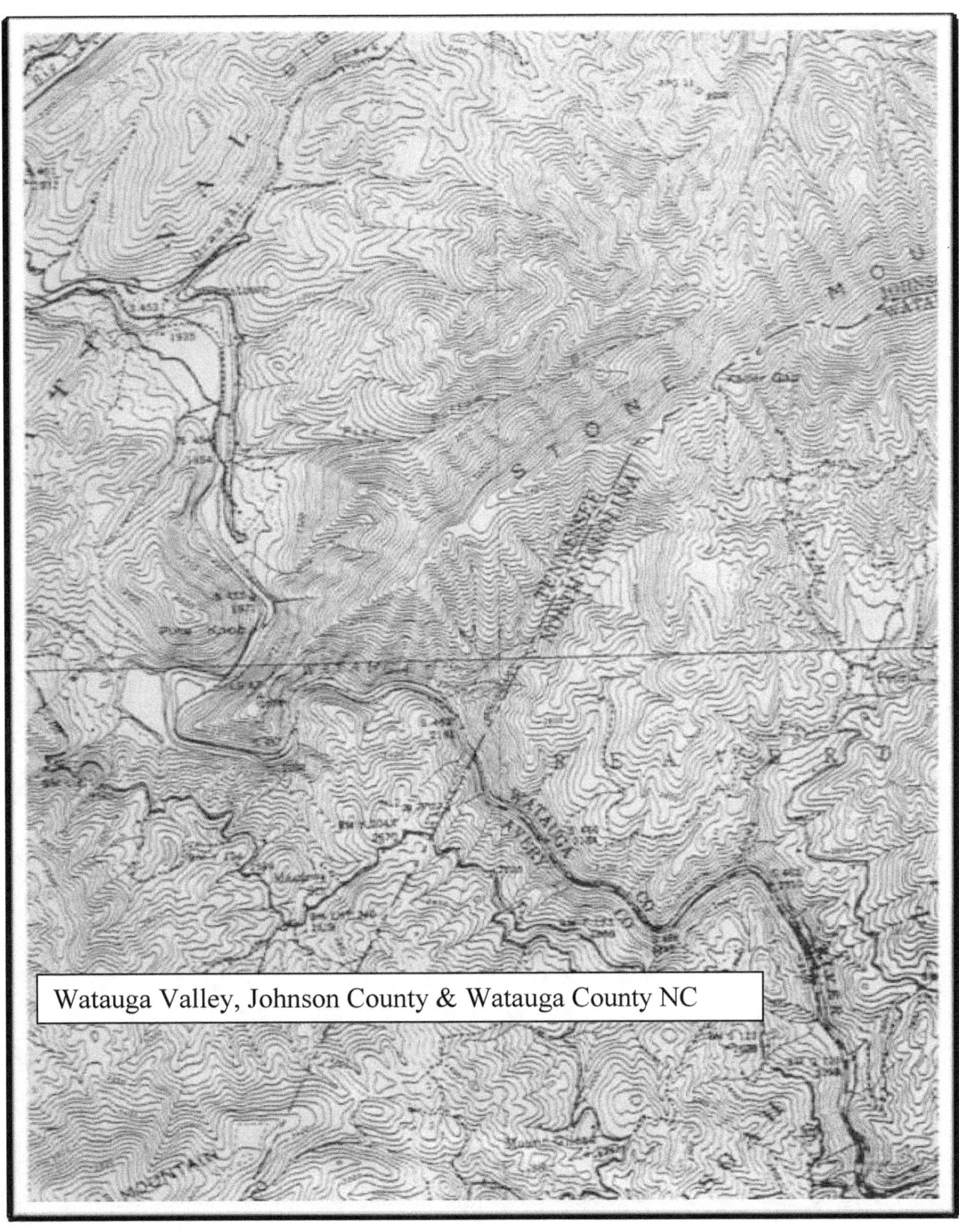
Watauga Valley, Johnson County & Watauga County NC

www.ingramcontent.com/pod-product-compliance
Lightning Source LLC
Chambersburg PA
CBHW080539230426
43663CB00015B/2645